More Praise for
THE RIGHT MOUNTAIN

"This book is very special."

—Dini Petty
The Dini Petty Show

"I was having a rather dreary, non-motivated, end-of-summer, no-holidays-planned, should-I-change-my-job sort of day. Browsing through a local bookshop, I picked up *The Right Mountain* and spent the evening reading it. Thank you. What a lovely inspirational story!"

—Jennifer Neal
London, England

"What a book! *The Right Mountain* gave me such huge pause for thought."

—Katy Peach Jones
Toronto, Ontario

"I have just finished reading *The Right Mountain* and had to write and thank you for writing such a great book. I am a mountaineering book collector, bookseller, and climber and have read just about every book written on Everest. Yours is so refreshing, so unlike all of the others, and so thought-provoking that I will be asking my climbing teammates to read it."

—Greg Glade
Top of the World Mountaineering & Polar Books
Williston, Vermont

"Experiential education at its best! Jim's story pushes us to extend ourselves, to grow, to dream. And he points out the difference between our dreams for ourselves and those others have for us. A valuable lesson."

—Wendy Pieh
Former Program and Executive Director
Outward Bound

"WOW! My husband and I just finished reading *The Right Mountain* and are inspired to purchase two additional copies for our friends."

—Sandy Neufeld
Delta, British Columbia

"There is no better motivational message about team building, knowing yourself, and defining success for your life than *The Right Mountain*. Jim's message empowers your people to accomplish their business and personal goals."

—Thomas P. Seay
Executive Vice-President
Wal-Mart Stores, Inc.

"It is impossible to read *The Right Mountain* without reflecting on your own life. I enjoyed this book immensely."

—Dr. Leonard Berry
Marketing Professor, Texas A&M
University, and Author of *On Great Service*

"Great story...great message! There are lessons here for everyone in the family and many at work. I want them all to read it. It's the kind of book I like to keep on my bedside table for regular referral. It will help me squeeze that little bit more out of life."

> —John M. Thompson
> Senior Vice-President and Group Executive
> IBM

"Your book is an incredible inspiration to me."

> —Diane Chesla
> Milton, Ontario

"A marvellous guide to our own inner journeys . . . with an insightful way of measuring success."

> —Reverend Chris Lehman
> United Church of Canada

"I took *The Right Mountain* home and read it cover to cover the following afternoon. The book was easy to read, which made it that much harder to put down. Thank you for recharging my batteries and reminding me of some of the basics that we all forget too quickly."

> —Dick Smeelen
> Toronto, Ontario

"I read your book in an evening. What an enjoyable book."

> —Steve Aho
> Kitchener, Ontario

"*The Right Mountain* is a compelling and inspirational book."

> —Peter Williams
> President
> Equitable Life of Canada

"Your book, right from the preface, put my life and goals into perspective. I would like to thank you for placing your feelings, goals, and successes in words. This way people like myself can learn to realize what their 'core values' are in life."

> —Sue Edmiston
> Shawnee, Kansas

"A book that first captures the heart and then goes on to snare the mind. The lessons go down easy, but they refuse to go away . . . . If there is an unclimbed Mount Everest in your life, I highly recommend this book. It will first help you decide if you're on the right mountain; and then it will guide you to the top."

> —H. John Greeniaus
> President & CEO
> Nabisco, Inc.

THE
RIGHT
MOUNTAIN

Success. It's one of the most alluring words in our vocabulary. We dream about it. Plan for it. Chase after it. But just what is it we're after? What really defines success?

We all need to have our own definition of success. Either we come to terms with that definition, or we risk paying the price: Career crises. Broken marriages. Bankruptcies. Even death . . . .

It happened in 1988, and a man named Jim Hayhurst was there to witness it. Two men died trying to climb Mount Everest. They died because they failed to understand themselves and their goals. They attempted a climb that was not for them. They were not on the right mountain.

The Right Mountain is Jim's story of that climb. But more than an adventure story, *The Right Mountain* is a graphic illustration of what it means to be successful. Not just in terms of short-lived victories. But in terms that are right for the individual, that lead to sustained success and real personal satisfaction.

This expedition will take you across surging rivers, over treacherous ice fields, and up the world's highest mountain, where temperatures dip to 60 below and winds gust to over 160 miles per hour. A place where teamwork, commitment, and self-awareness take on stark new meaning in the face of adversity, and even death.

Through *The Right Mountain*, Everest becomes a striking metaphor, teaching powerful lessons for personal growth.

THE
RIGHT
MOUNTAIN

Lessons From Everest
On the Real Meaning of Success

Jim Hayhurst, Sr.

John Wiley & Sons

Toronto • New York • Chichester • Brisbane • Singapore

Copyright© 1997 Jim Hayhurst, Sr.

John Wiley & Sons Canada, Ltd

22 Worcester Road
Etobicoke, Ontario
M9W 1L1

Canadian Cataloguing in Publication Data

Hayhurst, Jim
    The right mountain: lessons from Everest on the real meaning of success

ISBN 0-471-64150-2 (bound)   ISBN 0-471-64220-7 (pbk.)

1. Success   2. Motivation (Psychology).
3. Mountaineering–Everest, Mount (China and Nepal). I. Title

BF637.S8H3   158'.I   C95-932531-X

Production Credits

Cover & text design: Christine Rae
Electronic Assembly: Christine Rae
Printer: Tri-graphic Printing Ltd.
Photo Credits: Jim Hayhurst, Sr.; Jim Hayhurst, Jr.; Members of the 1988 Canadian Everest Expedition Team; Jim Elzinga, leader of the 1986 Canadian Everest Expedition

Printed and bound in Canada
10 9 8 7 6 5

CONTENTS

PROLOGUE

Climb Mount Everest?

"Would you like to go to Everest?" Jim Elzinga asked.

"Um, thanks, uh, could I think about it?" I replied.

I hung up the phone. It was September 1985. I was forty-four years old, the father of three teenage kids, a husband, and I was looking for a new focus for my life. Three months earlier my partners and I had sold Hayhurst Advertising, one of the three largest advertising agencies in Canada, and a vital member of an international network of agencies. We sold because we couldn't get the international group to commit to a common goal.

I was looking for a new challenge.

But *Everest?*

I had done some climbing as a result of my involvement in Outward Bound, the world-wide leader in the use of natural obstacles like mountains and rivers as devices to increase self-esteem and self-confidence. In fact, I had just become Chairman of Outward Bound Canada, a volunteer position, and a few weeks before had been climbing up and rappelling down some mountains in British Columbia. I was in decent shape for a man my age and I had done some mountain climbing, but nothing like. . . well, there is nothing like Everest.

Everest?

I love challenges. Some of my friends say I live for challenges. Tell me I can't do it and I'll probably give it a try. I'd always said that I didn't want to lie on my deathbed saying, "I wish I had. . . ."

But some risks may just be too great. I had once raced sports cars, but I stopped when a friend crashed in front of me. It took a year and many operations to rebuild his body and face. A successful driver needs to believe he will not crash. When Tommy crashed, I realized I could too. I lost that edge, that supreme confidence. I gave up racing.

But I continued to seek out new challenges. Three of us created a successful advertising campaign for Alberta Vodka by going to Russia in 1970, when it was still a very "closed" country, and sneaking photographs in Red Square of Russians drinking our vodka. The Canadian Embassy spirited us out of the country after we were chased by the Russian police.

I had been on cattle drives in Wyoming, Montana, and British Columbia. I had white-water rafted down the Green and Yampa Rivers which lead into Lake Powell, at the top of the Grand Canyon. There I had been caught in a whirlpool which, but for the strong arms of Judy Doverspike, would have drowned me.

I like adventure, risk, and challenge.

Everest. Was it too big a reach?

I decided it was. I decided not to go.

But I offered to be with the Everest team vicariously. I gave them office space in Toronto to serve as the eastern base for their fund raising. This was quickly accepted because, not surprisingly, the team members all lived in the west, where the mountains are, and most of the sponsorship money would probably come from the east, where corporate Canada lives. I watched them as they went through the ups and downs of training, tried to find financial sponsors, created an equipment list, and organized the myriad details involved in getting six tons of food and supplies into Tibet, a Communist-controlled country.

The Continental Bank eventually signed on as the major sponsor, contributing the majority of the $300,000 budget and, through its headquarters in Toronto, I kept in touch with the climb. Part of the deal with the bank was that the team radioed back regular reports on their progress, and the bank used the climb as the basis for a branch contest. Each branch set a loan and deposit target—their Everest—and as the Everest team reached new heights, the branches would attempt to keep up.

Seven weeks after the start of the climb, four members of the team were 27,000 feet up the north face of Everest and had a crack at the summit. Barry Blanchard and Dwayne Congdon were selected to make the attempt, leaving the other two, Sharon Wood and Kevin Doyle, as backups in case of emergencies. If all went well, Sharon and Kevin could attempt a summit the next day.

That night, the Canadian team learned that an American team was attempting Everest from the south side, and that their goal was to put a woman from their team on the top of Everest. She would thus become the first North American woman to reach the summit of Everest.

Barry and Sharon talked. The Canadians didn't want to miss the chance to put a woman on top before the Americans, but the sacrifice for someone to step aside would be huge. . . every professional climber wants to summit Everest. And this was Barry's chance. He knew he might never get another opportunity. Back and forth, back and forth, they discussed it. Then Barry made the call. . . he owed Sharon. He would step aside!

On May 25, 1986, Sharon Wood and Dwayne Congdon reached the top of Everest. But you not only have to get there, you have to get back. There were problems getting back down because they were exhausted and had lost all their supplies. A rescue team was sent up. Sharon and Dwayne were saved, but there was no chance for a second attempt. Barry had to come back down, without achieving his dream.

Barry had made the ultimate sacrifice for a mountain climber when he gave his spot to Sharon. And Sharon reaped the rewards of being the first North American woman to reach the peak. She is on the lecture circuit now, telling her story and helping others realize their potential. She relives the joy, utter exhaustion, and sense of relief through the slides and videos of her climb.

Everest. The ultimate challenge. I wasn't physically

there, but intellectually I had lived through the adventure time and time again. Al Wiggan, one of my business partners, ran a Hayhurst company in Calgary and had been a part of the climb with Sharon. Whenever we met, we talked about the climb, or at least he talked and I listened. I was fascinated and, I guess, a bit envious, for he had been a part of something extraordinary.

In November 1987, a year and a half after Sharon's summit, I got a call from Al. Barry Blanchard had a permit to climb Everest. He was building a team. He planned to have two primary climbers, Marc Twight and himself, and wanted about a dozen others for the support team.

Canada was going back to Everest. *Would I like to try out for the team?* I said I'd think about it. I wasn't sure whether to thank him or not. I wasn't sure I needed to go through the questions again. I was two years older.

All my previous discussions with Al flashed through my mind. Nine months of exhaustive training, the thrill of the summit for the team, the near-deaths along the way as glaciers collapsed and individuals pushed themselves beyond their limits. And I remembered how Barry had given Sharon the chance to be number one. I shared his exhilaration at getting another chance.

I searched my mind for the lessons of the 1986 climb. I knew it was a team sport and that others would depend upon my strength, both physical and mental.

I wouldn't be able to quit or let go. Everything would be a matter of life and death, black and white. I envisioned trekking, then climbing. Climbing in weather so cold, with winds so strong, that even the time I had spent in the Arctic wasn't a good comparison. There, in Whale Cove, on the northwestern shores of Hudson's Bay, it was so cold that even huge gas blow heaters were unable to thaw our small airplane's engine. I knew that Everest was colder, and that there would be no snowmobile to take me back to a warm cabin.

I couldn't do it. It was too overwhelming. I just couldn't give as much as Everest would demand.

I phoned Barry Blanchard, the leader of the expedition dubbed *Everest Express*, and said, "No, no thanks. But thanks for thinking of me. Good luck!" After I hung up, I wondered if it was the right decision, if I would lie on my deathbed saying, "I wish I had tried Everest." Here I was, sitting in my den at home, secure in my comforts, saying no to what, probably, at my age, would be my last big physical challenge.

Just then, Jimmy, our 20-year-old son who had been listening to the phone call, said, "So, they're going back to Everest."

"Yes," I said quietly.

"And you're not going?"

"No, I'm not."

"Well," he said, "if you're not going, maybe I could?"

"Jimmy," I said, "I don't think you just *go* to Everest. It's bigger than that."

He paused, "Well, could I at least try out for the team?"

What a great lesson that might be! He'd done some rock climbing, some mountain work, but he didn't seem to sense the enormity of Everest. Maybe the tryouts would expose him to real challenge and the experiential learning that comes from a physical challenge attempted, even if not completed—especially if not completed. He was an accomplished athlete, but perhaps things had come a little easily for him due to his physical strength and co-ordination. This might just be the challenge to make him stretch.

"I'll call Barry Blanchard back. We'll ask him," I said.

I got Barry on the phone again. Jimmy picked up the extension and I introduced him to Barry. The two of them talked.

"Do you know much about Everest?" Barry asked.

Jimmy had to admit that, no, he really didn't.

"Well," said Barry, "there are three ways that you can die. First, you can die of cerebral edema, where the inside of your head implodes down your spinal chord." Jimmy rolled his shoulders, trying to visualize the experience. He shook his head and said, "What's the second way?"

"You can die of pulmonary edema, where the liquid gathers in your lungs, and as you breathe, you gurgle, and as you gurgle, you drown."

Jimmy swallowed. "And the third way?"

"You can fall off the side," said Barry.

The telephone line was silent. "Why are you only telling me the downside?" Jimmy asked.

"Because most people visualize only the upside, the glory, the newspaper photos, and barroom stories. You have to understand the downside too, before you make a commitment to something big, like Everest."

I listened on the extension. It sounded like a metaphor for life. You have to recognize the downside, the consequences, the risks, before you take on a project. That's why in business plans there is a section called *Risks and Offsets* where comparisons between the benefits, the profits, and the costs or losses are made and quantified on the way to a final go or no-go decision.

"Do you still want to try out?" Barry asked.

Jimmy paused, but only briefly. "Yes, I do."

And that's when my wife, Sue, knew there were two idiots in our family.

This book tells the story of the next eleven months of our lives. It also tells of some of the things I learned on the trip about myself. I saw metaphors for life in many of our situations, and the sheer scope of Everest, I felt, dramatized those messages.

When I started talking publicly about my experiences and the ideas in this book, I was far from the mainstream of business theory and, frankly, from the theories of most motivational speakers, including those who had climbed Everest. Typically, the thesis was "You can do it, just try harder, do it, suck it up, reach for the top." Most people were still talking about the American Dream, reaching the top, becoming a millionaire, having power, prestige, and status. Being a success!

Michael Milken epitomized that dream. In one year he made more money than McDonald's Corporation worldwide. Ben Johnson was at the top of the athletic world after he won the gold medal in the 100-metre sprint at the 1988 Olympics in Seoul.

Then Michael went to jail for insider trading. And Ben, well, he had taken steroids to enhance his performance, and in the random drug tests after the race, he'd been caught. We found out he had made a deal with the devil. He gave away his body in return for the very temporary ownership of a gold medal. Initially both Michael and Ben were successes and then, overnight, they weren't. And what about O.J. Simpson, Richard Nixon, Donald Trump, Elvis? Success. What is the definition of success? How do *you* define it?

People have started to question the American Dream of *success at any price*. They are learning what I had learned in my encounter with Everest: that we need to stop, think, figure out our priorities in life, not just proceed at any cost. We need to define, quite specifically, the word *success*, for ourselves, both long-term and short-term.

Clearly the "money and material wealth at any cost" definition of success is being re-evaluated as we approach the 21st century. We are all grappling with how to cope with the changes that are affecting our jobs, careers, marriages, children, and communities, and still feel *successful*. In the past two decades, many parents have turned over the raising of their children to their schools and communities in order to pursue careers. But now some of them are questioning their definition of success and asking, "What about love, time, and energy for the kids?"

Slowly we are returning to the concept of taking responsibility for ourselves and those we bring into this world, and this happens to coincide with the new corporate reality. Historically, an organization hired employees for life, planned their careers, looked after their benefits, and even provided for their retirement. The employee didn't have to do anything, didn't have to plan: just turn up and do the job.

The nineties saw an end to that. No more jobs for life, no more huge benefit plans. In fact, no more jobs. Now projects, assignments, one-year contracts, outsourcing, and consulting are the terms of employment. "Oh, and by the way, you are responsible for your own benefit plans. We, the corporation, don't do that anymore." In fact, government pension plans are underfunded, so don't count on them either.

There is no corporate ladder to climb, no promotion, no titles, no outside demonstration of success. After twelve or thirteen years of school, three, four or more years of college, where the teacher always told us how we were doing, where the assignments were clearly outlined, where the next step was obvious, we have reached a chasm. There is no obvious next step, no one to tell us what to do next or how to do it, no one to mark our performance.

We have to decide for ourselves what our goals are, what our definition of *success* is. We have to take total responsibility for ourselves.

Everest was a new world for Jimmy and me. And this book attempts to describe the adventure. But it is more than just a story; it is a metaphor for life. And it is also a workbook.

If you think you will want to use it as a workbook, turn now to page 181. Write your definition of *success* in the space provided. Don't spend hours on it; just briefly jot down the words or phrases that define how you look at life. To help you do this, imagine you are able to listen in on your friends and workplace associates after you have died, or on your 85th birthday. What are they saying about you? What do you wish they were saying? Their words, the way they describe you, the way you want them to describe you, may be your definition of *success*. Be precise, be succinct. Try it.

After you have read the book, we'll do some exercises to review that definition and to give you a template to test your life's decisions against.

For those of you who just want an adventure without a lot of soul-searching, enjoy the book. It was quite a trip!

CHAPTER 1

The Everest Express Team Tryouts

*T*he tryouts for the 1988 Everest Express Team were set for late November 1987 in Calgary, Alberta. Barry Blanchard invited Jimmy to the tryouts. Jimmy was at King's University in Halifax at the time. He received permission to miss two weeks of school and, in fact, if he made the team, he had permission to miss the entire first two months of the next year. (The school deserves a lot of credit for recognizing the educational value of this experience.) He flew to Calgary. I went along to protect my little (6'2" and 195 pound) boy.

When we arrived in Calgary at about 9:00 p.m., a couple of team members met us at the airport. They drove us to a restaurant, where the other guys trying out for the team were having dinner. We were introduced, served drinks, and the conversation continued. It was obvious that they each knew at least one or two of the other participants and it took a while for us to fit in — but our common experiences eased the tension. I noticed that this time there were no women trying out for the team — no Sharon Woods.

Jimmy was the youngest by at least two or three years and I the oldest by three or four years. The others seemed to have all had climbing experience in the Rockies. Most were in business, several in their own businesses which, in retrospect, made sense, because they could take the time off for the climb without asking their bosses' permission. To me they seemed young, strong, and all had that outdoor look. Jimmy appeared quite comfortable with them and his physical size and obvious confidence overcame the lack of shared experiences.

My Outward Bound experience and Jimmy's camping and climbing experience in the Adirondacks were easy connectors with our western companions and soon we were swapping stories. The wine and beer increased the decibel level of the adventures and the camaraderie. At about one in the morning, they rolled us into our hotel beds, promising, in what I later realized were relatively sober voices, that they'd wake us up early for a workout.

Four hours later, through the haze of booze, we heard people pounding on our door. Shaking our throbbing heads, we opened the door to find our "teammates" in full climbing gear ready to work out!

At 5:12 a.m., badly hung over and seriously out of shape, we were driven to the bottom of "the stairs," 149 steps that lead from the Bow River to the north plateau in Calgary. When climbers are in Calgary, this is their workout area. For others, it is just a way to get from one side of town to the other through a park on either side of the river.

Barry, in full climbing gear, with a pack on his back, started running up "the stairs." Others, in various levels of climbing attire, followed. Jimmy and I were in shorts, sweatshirts, and runners and in deep need of sleep, water, and aspirin. Jimmy, with barely a glance at me, fell in behind the other dozen guys and started trotting up "the stairs." I sidled over to the bottom, gingerly took the first step and slowly walked up the 149 (yep, I counted them) steps.

Four hours later, Barry had done one hundred "reps" (repetitions—up and down is one rep). Jimmy had done twenty-eight reps. I was stuck at the top. I had done eleven-and-a-half reps.

At the top, on the eleventh cycle, my left leg cramped. I couldn't put any weight on it. I couldn't get back down. I could hardly stand. I called for help. A couple of guys drove a car around the back side of the hill and picked me up. One hour later, my legs still shook so much I couldn't even go down the three steps into a hot tub. They lifted me in!

Slowly my muscles relaxed and I joined in the conversation in the hot tub. I thanked them very much for last night's welcome and noted that, in retrospect, they had seemed to re-order drinks frequently for us while they slowly sipped theirs.

They laughed. "Congratulations on your observation skills," one of them remarked. "They can be very useful on a mountain. But we weren't just trying to make you suffer. The only simulation for climbing at altitude is a serious hangover. You feel nauseous, you get headaches, and your throat and mouth are dry. The only difference is that the hangover probably will recede in six to ten hours, while on the mountain, the feeling lasts as long as you are at altitude. You come from Toronto, which is basically at sea level, and even though we live in Calgary at 3,341 feet, the Himalayas are over 15,000 feet—we'll all have a tough time adjusting."

The only

simulation for

climbing at altitude

is a serious hangover.

"There's another reason not to go to Everest!" I said to Jimmy.

The next day eight of those trying out for the support team, including Jimmy, went to Montana to do some climbing. Although Barry wouldn't be with them, it was a chance for them to learn a lot about each other. I didn't go; I wasn't really trying out for the team anyway.

Barry had already lined up the primary support team—those that were necessary for the success of the climb past Base Camp. I asked him what he was looking for as he put together this secondary support group. He said that in building any team, he looked for three things in each individual.

"First, does he have the *skills?* Can he use an ice axe and carabiners; can he tie knots, rappel?

Does he have the skills?

"Second, does he have a real *interest* in this climb? Is this just a lark for him, a college prank? Is he committed, truly committed? Will he give his all and then some?

A real interest?

"Third, does he have the right *values?* Is he a team player or will he put his personal goals ahead of the team's? Will he look out for himself when he's hanging on the rope with others below him? Will he go on and break the trail, set pitons for others, back-breaking, arm-tearing work, which might drain him and leave him too exhausted to go for the top? Or will he hold back, not do at least his share on the way up, so that he'll be in the best shape of all to go for the top? Will he give that extra little bit when lives are at stake?"

The right values?

I stayed in the west, doing some consulting in Vancouver, until they returned. After ten days of climbing, talking, biking, running, being pushed to the limit, and then a little more, sharing and learning, the group returned to Calgary.

The next day Barry invited Jimmy, at twenty years old, to be the youngest member of the Everest Express Team.

And me, at forty-seven, to be the oldest.

Barry had chosen carefully. He wanted team players, guys who would sacrifice their chance at glory, at the peak of the mountain, to help others. (Just as he had done in 1986.) He wanted individuals who could and would talk about issues bothering them, rather than internalizing them, and letting them come to a boil later when it was tougher to defuse them. He wanted people who could adjust to change, often dramatic change, quickly and confidently, without time-consuming cajoling.

He wanted individuals who could operate under intense physical and emotional pressure, in life-and-death situations, and still be able to function at an elite level. And he wanted individuals who were entrepreneurs, quick and positive thinkers, and risk-takers. He knew not everyone would be there for the final assault. There would be two primary climbers, Marc and himself. They would rely on the rest of us as support to assist them in getting supplies up to the camp at 21,000 feet, from where they planned to make their four-day assault (three days up and one down) on the summit. He wanted to be sure he could trust the skills and values of whoever was there.

Interestingly, for many of us, *skills, interests,* and *values* are the attributes we want in friends, spouses, organizations, and peer groups. Yet we don't always articulate these needs as we make decisions. Maybe we should.

Building A Team, A Real Team

The three key components required when building an Everest team — in fact, any team — are: technical skills, a real interest in taking on the challenge at hand, and a common set of values.

CHAPTER 2

We're All In This Together

I liked challenge,

but perhaps this was too

big a challenge?

On the flight back to Toronto, Jimmy and I talked about Everest. Neither of us had accepted the offer yet, but Jimmy was bubbling, thrilled at being asked to join the team!

I, too, was overwhelmed. I was forty-seven, had completed about one-tenth the number of reps on "the stairs" that Barry had, with no equipment, no weight on my back; I had seized up and had to be helped off the Calgary plateau. How could I consider a mountain, let alone The Mountain?

I was scared. Sure, I liked challenge, but perhaps this was too big a challenge? I worried about my age; my back, which goes out about twice a year; my weight, which was about 15 pounds above ideal; and my skinny legs. On the other hand, my ego was being challenged! I didn't want my son to think I was a wimp. Maybe I could do it?

I struggled to find balance between machismo and sanity, between ego and reality. But Jimmy's enthusiasm was overwhelming. "What a great father-son experience," he exclaimed. "We can do it!"

By the time the plane had landed in Toronto, I had cautiously agreed to undergo a major physical examination, to see if I should even consider such an adventure. Our youngest daughter, Barbara, had a good friend, Sarah, whose father, Dr. Chuck Bull, was the doctor for the Canada Cup Hockey Team. He would know how to test someone who wanted to be part of an elite team.

A couple of days later I called Chuck. He didn't laugh (out loud) and agreed to set up a test for me.

The next Wednesday morning, a forty-seven year-old business executive, who spent a lot of time in planes, at restaurants, and at a desk, who lived on a farm, cut some wood, threw some hay bales, built some fences, and played a little golf, hopped on the stationary bicycle at The Fitness Institute.

Electrodes were attached to my body, nurses stood by the monitors and I began pedalling. I pedalled. They increased the brake pressure. I pedalled. The brake pressure was increased again. I saw stars.

When I woke up, I was lying on the exercise pad beside the bike. I had fainted. I looked up. The nurses were reviewing the tape from the monitors, scanning the results, drawing conclusions, talking among themselves, completely oblivious to me.

I stood up. The doctor turned to me. "That was great!" he said. "Let's do it again!"

I sagged. "Oh, sure. I feel as if I almost died. And you say let's do it again?"

"We have to," he said. "We have to find your recovery rate."

"What about a case of beer?" I ventured.

"Get back on the bike, Mr. Everest."

I got back on the bike. They hooked up the electrodes. I started pedalling. They increased the brake pressure.

When I woke up this time, I was lying in the doctor's office. I had nicked my head when I fell off the bike. They were patching me up.

As I staggered out of the office, the nurses turned from the monitors to stare at my skinny legs. Obviously the "Mr. Everest" had been explained to them.

The doctor, noticing my embarrassment at the stares, intervened. "There's good news about those skinny legs."

"What?" I asked.

"They won't cause much wind resistance."

"Thanks," I murmured to the sound of giggles. "Seriously, what are my chances of going to Everest?"

"Possible, just possible. But only if you are prepared to commit to a training program."

Commit sounded like a threat. I asked him what he meant.

"It means we have nine months before the team leaves and I'll need you at The Fitness Institute two hours a night, four nights a week, and eight to ten hours each day on the weekend. I'll need you without fail. You need to go full tilt, under the leadership of a trainer. You'll do everything he or she says, extending yourself all the time. Your body will scream and your mind will bend, but you can't ease off one bit. You have to give more every time you feel you've reached the end. You can't complain. Not even once. Not even silently. And you have to give up booze. None, not a

Commit sounded

like a threat.

drop, not at Christmas, not on your birthday, not ever. That's what I mean by *commit*."

I sank to the mat.

I'd played football, hockey, and done some swimming in high school, and competed in the same sports at the inter-faculty level at university. I was in as good shape as most of my buddies and peers, but could I *commit* to this?

I had just started a new business, The Hayhurst Career Centre, and it needed lots of attention. This training would mean that I would get up, work out, go to work, work out, go to bed. Get up. . . . There would be no free time. I'd sleep, work, work out, and eat. Nothing else.

No time for my wife, my kids, my friends. No overtime at the office if there was a panic. Because my life, and the lives of others on the Everest team, depended on my fitness.

But I soon realized it wasn't just me that was going to have to commit. Everyone else who was a part of my life would have to commit as well. If they couldn't understand why I couldn't be with them, if they wondered why I wasn't carrying my share of the load at home, at the office, socially, they would undermine my resolve. They had to commit too, and not demand my time or my energy. If they nagged, I'd have divided loyalties, and I would lose my focus and my resolve.

That evening I talked to Sue, or Swebbs as I call her. Would she support me as I started to train?

Could I commit to this?

Would she be there for the kids? I talked to our other two kids, Boo (Barbara), eighteen, and Cid (Cindy), twenty-three. Would they understand that I wouldn't be able to spend much time with them? Boo was in boarding school and Cid was graduating from university, so they were both on their own, but we had always been a close family, and I had always been available.

"the ultimate

father-son

experience"

Jimmy and I talked about the downsides as well as the upsides of the "ultimate father-son experience." Could we accept it if the other failed? What would be a failure? What if one of us got hurt, would the other have to stay with him? What if one of us died? What if we disagreed on a strategy or technique on the mountain? What if one of us just wanted to quit, would the other forever look down on him? We talked and talked. We even wrote independent magazine articles on the prospect of climbing Everest which, when we read each other's, were comfortingly similar. We felt we could do it.

I talked to many of our friends. Some laughed, some were incredulous, many thought I was just plain nuts.

I talked to Gay Marshall and Ian Cameron who worked with me at The Hayhurst Career Centre. It was a personal service business, but I was going to be available only 8:30 a.m. to 6:00 p.m., Monday to Friday, not just for our clients, but for Gay and Ian too.

Everyone bought in; they understood what I was trying to do, even if they didn't understand why. They agreed to pick up my responsibilities and to support, not nag. We all *committed*.

Commitment

Nothing significant is achieved without commitment. And it is a shared commitment that makes the difficult possible. Involve others in the commitment.

CHAPTER 3

"I'm Training for Everest
and Having a Little Trouble
On This Hill!"

I thought my life had been full before. I didn't think I had any spare time. In fact, I didn't. I just had to add more waking hours to my day.

The morning after the testing, I woke up at 5:00 a.m. The sun was just starting to rise. It was a clear, cool morning. I realized that this was the first day of the rest of my life. I would be forever changed, whether I gave up that morning, climbed the mountain or anything in between. Things would never be the same. I felt intimidated by my own decision to try this climb and all it entailed.

I dressed in warm clothes, pulled on what I hoped would be my lucky toque and went out to my new 13-gear mountain bike. The farm dogs, Pal the Lab, and Parker the German Shepherd, were surprised to see me, but didn't offer to join me as I headed down the laneway. I felt good, it was a great day and I was off on a new adventure.

Initially, the most intimidating aspect was the length of the training period, nine months, and the length of the climb, seven weeks. I have a short attention span, like a Labrador puppy, and I hate to train. I like the game day, not the practice day. This was a new game. Could I keep focused? Could I keep committed?

There is a big, long hill near our farm, about a 300-foot vertical drop and a quarter mile horizontial ride. This was my test hill. Could I ride up it? I started in lowest gear. It was tough. I started puffing. Two-thirds of the way up I saw stars. I slid off the bike. My

Could I keep focused?

Could I keep committed?

vision narrowed. I panicked. I tried to regulate my breathing, to breathe deeply. Nothing happened. I was reeling, falling down and gasping. A car drove by, stopped, looked, then continued on. I thought of waving the driver over, or trying to, but what would I say, even if I could talk? "I'm training for Everest. . . but I'm having a little trouble on this hill?"

In what was, I'm sure, less than two minutes, my breathing slowed, my gasps became deep breaths, and I could stand up. I was going to live. But I had a long way to go, before even thinking of Everest. The gap between me now and someone capable of going to Everest was the width of the Grand Canyon. It seemed impossible. I rode home, showered and went to work.

I had to think this through. On the very first day, I was totally overwhelmed by what lay ahead. How could I keep going through nine months of elite physical training, pushing my body and my mind, when on the first day, on the first little hill, I thought I'd die? I second-guessed myself all day.

At the end of the day, I fell back on the true motivation for doing this—the father-son experience. Perhaps to show him that I could do it. Perhaps just to be with him. Perhaps, although in retrospect this was naive, to help him. I've always encouraged our kids to be curious, to try. I love them and it seems I'll do almost anything to be with them, to help them grow. This was the test of "almost anything."

That first day, I left my office at 7:00 p.m. and

drove to The Fitness Institute. They'd offered to provide personal trainers, the facilities, and an individual program in return for my giving a presentation to their members on my return. (Thanks, John Wildman.) I started slowly, but the trainers pushed. A little faster, a little deeper, a little, a little. They had a good sense of what I could do and a great sense of how to make me give a little more.

The stationary bike, the rowing machine, hydra weights, and the dreaded Stairmaster. I worked out until 10:00 p.m., then showered, drove home to the farm, ate, and slept. The next day, I would wake up, do it again.

It was hell. But every morning and every night I was back at it. In good weather I'd ride my bike up and down hills at the farm between 6:00 and 7:00 in the morning. I'd be at the office by 9:00, leave around 7:00 in the evening to go to The Fitness Institute.

I knew the trainers were working on my physical strength, especially my lower back, where I've always had problems, but also on my legs, arms, and shoulders.

I also knew they were working on my cardiovascular and cardiopulmonary systems. As you climb through about 12,000 feet, the air pressure and oxygen decrease is exponential. At 18,000 feet, the oxygen content in the air is half that at sea level. You have to suck in twice the volume of air to get the same amount of oxygen. And, the higher you go, the greater the volume required. So, to get enough oxygen to survive, notwithstanding the oxygen demands that physical exertion puts on the system, you have to increase your cardiovascular capacity and strength. Imagine puffing and puffing, really hard, for two minutes. That takes muscle and is tiring. Now imagine it for days, for weeks. That's the muscle they were working on. And because you are working so hard at altitude, the capacity of the lungs must be increased as well.

What I didn't know was that they were also working on my head, my brain, my mind, my *mental attitude.* Because on the mountain and, frankly, in the rest of life, it is our *attitude* that either makes or breaks us. They had to prove to me that I could do much more than I thought I could. And when I believed that, they had to extend me again, so that, eventually, I would believe in myself enough that I could keep going when all my physical signals were overloaded.

Every two months, the doctor would take me back into the testing room, hook up the electrodes, and make me pedal. Then he would test me, evaluate the results, and change my training program. And then I'd go into withdrawal. Just as I was beginning to feel that I could do the last program, they would change it. I knew I'd never do the new one, which was longer, deeper, harder. But I had to. *Attitude.*

Finally I understood what my trainers were doing. They knew that on the mountain things would change—weather, plans, roles, strengths, everything— nothing would be constant or predictable. They knew

They were

building

my attitude.

that no one would have the time to cajole me to go on; I'd have to be able to do that myself. They were training me to pick myself up and keep on going, mentally. They were building my *attitude.*

But knowing why they kept changing the program didn't make it any easier. I would still ask for an explanation of the changes, for support, for proof that this program was better. Just talk to me!

They wouldn't. They left me on my own. Slowly I'd try the new program; slowly I'd pick myself up.

Basically, at The Fitness Institute, I was working with four pieces of equipment. The Stairmaster worked on my cardiovascular and my legs. The rowing machine worked on my cardiovascular, my legs, my upper body and my lower back. The hydra weights worked on my upper body and legs. The stationary bicycle worked on my legs and cardiovascular. I also did stretching exercises, a little bit of running on their indoor track, and swam laps and did stretches in the pool.

I had a two-hour program. I would ride the bicycle at a particular speed and tension for 20 minutes, then stretch, then lift weights for 20 minutes, then jog, then row at a tension level for 30 minutes, then a short jog, then use the Stairmaster at a prescribed level for 20 minutes, then a long, slow stretch.

Day after day I would do this, in conjunction with my early morning rides, and swimming at home. And ten hours each day of the weekend. Then two months later, they'd change it all again. I'd go into a funk. They would increase the tension level, increase the weights, and increase the speed.

The changes got more severe. I'd pout longer, consider the options of quitting, getting another trainer who would talk to me, explain why, and support me. But I never missed a day. I knew if I stopped once, I'd stop again.

By mid-July, I knew I had made progress. I could ride up that infamous hill at the farm in top gear! In office buildings, I ran up the stairs to the top floors. I felt great. And I started feeling confident! My mind was strong. I could focus. I could keep going when my legs, my arms, my chest, said no, no more. I was getting stronger, physically and mentally. By late August, I was feeling even better. I felt I could handle anything my trainer threw at me. I had lost twenty pounds of fat and I had put on ten pounds of muscle. I had definition in my thighs!

The week before we were to leave, I treated myself to a deep, hour-long massage. Halfway through the massage, I felt a twinge. The masseur triggered a back spasm! I'd spent nine months training, following a carefully crafted program that had me in the shape of my life, but now I had a spasm! I'd had them before and the routine was always the same: either spend two weeks in bed in the fetal position, or fourteen days visiting the chiropractor.

But the team was leaving in one week.

Fortunately, as a result of all my training and perhaps my mental strength, my back was fine in five days. The doctor and the trainers pronounced me fit

I felt great.

My mind was strong.

I could focus.

and ready to go. (Thanks, folks, for showing me what I could do. And thanks for your understanding of the human body and mind.)

Body And Mind

You need them both. Mountain climbing, like most things in life, is 80% mental and 20% physical. Your attitude is the real determinant of your ability to achieve your goals in life.

CHAPTER 4

Stairs and Beer

Versus

The Fitness Institute

*D*uring most of the time I was training, Jimmy was at university. I phoned regularly to ask how his training program was going.

"Fine," he'd say.

I'd tell him what I was doing.

"I'm playing soccer and doing a lot of running," he'd say.

"How about your other muscles, your back and shoulders," I'd ask.

"No problem," he'd reply. "I'm feeling great."

I didn't realize it until later, but this was his first step in defining his independence on this climb. He was going to do it his way. He supported me and encouraged me in my program, but he felt he knew what was best for him.

He was going to

do it his way.

To the best of my knowledge, his training program consisted of carrying a couple of cases of beer up to the fifteenth floor of his apartment building, emptying the bottles with some buddies, and then carrying the empties back down the stairs.

He was also playing university level soccer. And he was 21 years old. I thought he should train like me, but he didn't have to.

And it was not just age that made the difference. Sure we were different ages and needed different skill and muscle development, but we also operated in different ways. I didn't know how to train or retrain my body. Jimmy was much more aware of his body and so felt confident in his program.

In the home, in jobs, in schools, we have to recognize and celebrate these differences.

Everyone is different. Our schools think we should all be taught the same way, but some of us learn better reading and some listening; some in groups, some alone. We all have different skills, different experiences and different expectations, and we come with different levels of expertise.

As a boss, as a parent, as a teammate, as a friend, you shouldn't automatically apply your needs to others.

Jimmy spent that summer at Kilcoo Camp in northern Ontario as a section director. He was outdoors, swimming and running. All the staff and kids knew he was training for Everest, so he'd collect an entourage as he went out for his early morning run or swim. He was getting in shape his way.

At the end of August 1988, Jimmy and I flew to Vancouver, hooked up with the other twelve team members, flew to Hong Kong and then on to Kathmandu.

We were on our way to Everest!

Everybody Is Different

Recognize and celebrate these differences in

your family, your friends, and your associates.

CHAPTER 5

*You Don't Just **Go** To Everest*

At least, I thought we were going to Everest.

It turns out you don't go right to Everest, just as you don't go right to being a school principal, a sales manager, a pro golfer, or a parent. You acclimatize first, as a teacher, a sales rep, an amateur golfer, or during the nine months of gestation. You learn, you develop, and you get prepared.

Our plan was to trek the Annapurna Range of mountains to the west of Kathmandu, in a beautiful area below Maachupachare, or Fish-Tail Mountain (so called because of its shape). Maachupachare itself is a sacred mountain to the Nepalese, and is off-limits to all climbers. This trek would take us up to 13,000 feet, where we would begin our acclimatization, and still leave us time to get to Everest before winter brought plummeting temperatures and raging winds.

A bus took us to Pokhara about sixty miles west of Kathmandu, halfway to Maachupachare and dropped us in the middle of a schoolyard. It was pouring rain. Kids gathered around us as we unpacked the bus. Each of us had two packs: a small day-pack with a change of clothes, toiletries, and room for a water bottle and food; plus a full camping pack with the rest of our clothes and sleeping bags. Total weight, with everything in, about 80 pounds.

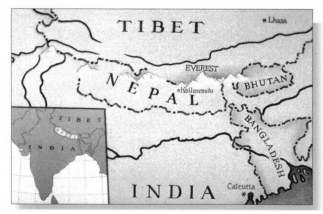

Our porters, about twelve of them, and their leader met us here. They were to carry our tents, our food, our medical supplies, our cooking utensils, as well as their meager personal supplies. They seemed to range in age from mid-teens to forty, but it was hard to tell. Only their leader spoke some English.

Our team sorted out the various packs with some degree of urgency. We wanted to get going. But the porters acted with a laconic, here-we-go-again, attitude.

When I was ready, I turned to the head porter and asked him where we were headed. He pointed up into the clouds at about two o'clock from the direction we were facing and said, "There — Maachupachare."

"How far is it?" I asked.

"Forty miles," he replied nonchalantly.

"Forty miles!" I gasped. "We are going to walk forty miles — and this is only the acclimatization!"

"That's as the bird flies," he noted. "We walk about sixty miles. . . there. . . and sixty miles back."

We were going to walk one hundred and twenty miles, from Toronto to London, Ontario, or New York to Philadelphia! I couldn't do it. I'd been training on the Stairmaster. *I hadn't actually walked anywhere!* On the very first day, before the very first step, I was again overwhelmed. All that training, all that suffering, all that deprivation, and now, before I'd even taken a step, I was ready to quit.

I realized that I had only two choices: Quit now. Or figure out a way to do it.

I remembered that failure is not the falling down, but the staying down.

I watched the rest of the team get ready to walk, picking up their packs, adjusting the straps. They were going to leave. None of them felt as overwhelmed as I did.

I decided I had to try. But I had to figure out quickly how I could do this. I remembered my training. Set an incremental goal; you don't have to do it all at once. Break the challenge into little pieces, little goals, and chew them off, one at a time. Go ahead, one step at a time. That's how you take on a huge challenge. I picked a curve in the road about a quarter mile ahead and set that as my goal.

Imagine buying a house, getting to be president, bringing up kids. It is hard to imagine when you are making $30,000 a year that you can save enough to buy a $300,000 house, let alone a cottage or a ski chalet as well. When you join an organization after college, the president's office and job look a long way away. And when your first child is just home from the hospital, how can you possibly get her from here to her wedding day?

One step at a time, with my head down, not looking at either the goal down the road, or the mountain in the distance, I set out. And when I got to the curve and was still alive, I set another incremental goal—the next curve.

One step at a time, one incremental goal after another, I set out. I knew I had two weeks of "acclimatizing" in front of me, and I was determined to give it my best shot.

Bite-Sized Pieces

When faced with an overwhelming challenge,

don't back away. Try to break it down into a

series of smaller achievable challenges. And

do it, one step at a time.

CHAPTER 6

High-Tech Climbers
and
Barefoot Porters

*W*hen Sir Edmund Hillary became the first person to reach the summit of Everest in May 1953, he had to contend not only with the mountain and the weather, but also with equipment. Cotton jackets and packs, leather boots, all soaked up moisture and doubled in weight. Leather boots froze and cracked, and leather straps on everything became brittle and tough to work with.

But on our climb, we had the most sophisticated, modern equipment money could buy. We had packs with straps that could shift the weight from one shoulder to the other, from the shoulders to the hips, from the hips back to the shoulders.

Our equipment was GORE-TEX nylon, space-age plastics, and all pieces were lightweight, non-moisture-absorbing, and durable.

We dressed in four layers: a silk or nylon underlayer to wick moisture away from our bodies to keep us dry and comfortable. This was topped by a wool or fleece layer for warmth and flexibility. Over this was a wind layer, usually GORE-TEX overalls and jacket. On the sleeves and collars of this jacket were wool patches, so we could wipe our dripping noses without freezing to the zippers on our jackets. All zippers had nylon pull straps, so they could be opened and closed while wearing mitts or gloves. The hoods of the jackets tied tight around our faces, leaving only a four-inch diameter hole to see and breathe through. The final layer was a down jacket, bulky when worn so we looked like the Michelin Man, but it rolled up into a ball smaller than a football for packing. These layers went on and off, depending upon the weather.

On the acclimatization climb, we spent a lot of time in shorts or light cotton slacks because the weather was warm in the lower levels of Nepal. We would wear thick wool socks, sometimes with a cotton or silk undersock to help prevent blisters, and hiking boots that also enabled us to pump an air cushion around blisters. These would also serve us well on the lower reaches of Everest, but once we got into snow and ice, we would switch to snowmobile-type boots: canvas or nylon tops with rubber soles and wool inner boots. These were comfortable yet warm for the pure hiking levels at altitude. When we got to vertical climbing areas, we would wear a ski-boot type of footwear consisting of a plastic outer shell which was very light, with a lace-up inner boot for stability and support. These, unlike ski-boots, were flexible and very light. Over them, went GORE-TEX gaiters to stop snow from getting into our boots. Crampons, a spiked sole much like telephone pole climbers use, were attached by straps to the outer shell when ice climbing was on the agenda.

We had two layers on our heads and hands. A nylon balaclava was covered by a wool balaclava. Our hands had a nylon glove covered by a wool mitt with GORE-TEX shell. When climbing ice, we wore plastic safety helmets.

Mountain climbers typically carry hundreds of feet of 5.5 mm thick nylon rope, carefully checked for abrasions that might rip and break; ice axes; pitons; carabiners; and jumars. Barry and Marc were planning to climb without ropes, harnesses, pitons, or ice screws — as pure a climb as possible!

While food was critical, it was also a nuisance. You

don't feel like eating at altitude and, of course, the oxygen decrease makes heating or cooking an issue. We carried gas stoves, canisters of fuel, and small pots to cook and to melt ice in for water. We wanted high energy food like gorp (raisins, nuts), cheese, boil-in-a-bag meals, and triple fudgeos (which I'll never eat again). All water had to be iodized for purity, so we masked it with fruit flavours.

Carl, our doctor, had a full medical kit, including a bunch of morphine for me in case my kidney stones re-occurred. (I'd had two attacks, six months apart, in the previous year and my sense was that if I got one on the mountain, I'd just throw myself over the side!) Carl had asked each of us for a list of special medical needs six months before the trip and we had all had exhaustive medicals, so he was, we hoped, prepared for anything. The fact that he was a veterinarian might have been a little disconcerting at first. But he was also a mountaineer with special mountain medical training. Also, we rationalized, his experience with patients who couldn't explain their problems would be an asset on the mountain where you hallucinate and are oxygen deprived, and therefore brain deprived!

Our porters didn't have quite the same equipment or support system. Their feet were bare and their clothes were little more than rags. They had wicker baskets in which they carried all our camping stuff: food, tents, medical supplies. When filled, the baskets each weighed more than eighty pounds and were carried only by a tump line that went from the bottom of the basket up across the porter's forehead and back down.

The porters were from the Kathmandu area and had been hired by a local outfitter that many of the expeditions use. All were male, lean, and almost lethargic in their attitude. I stared at them. They wouldn't make it; they weren't big enough, the loads we were asking them to carry were too heavy, and their equipment was primitive.

But I forgot about *motivation*. In this case, money was the key motivating factor. Nepal is an incredibly poor country; money from trekkers and climbers has a huge impact on the lives and lifestyles of the people there.

The early nineties have seen tremendous changes in corporate America. The big corporations like IBM and GM felt they were invincible, with their size, money, sophistication, and experience. But they, too, forgot about motivation: the motivation that drove Apple from a backyard business to the desks of millions; the motivation and creativity that the Japanese used to break the Big Three's stranglehold on the American car industry; the motivation that helped Ben & Jerry's, L.L. Bean, and hundreds of others to become major players in business. That same motivation helped create new schools, new teaching techniques, new medicines, the CD, the information highway, and new entertainment techniques.

Motivation is the key to achieving your dreams, your goals. But you must understand what it is that motivates you. Money, any money, is a lifesaver in many environments, as it is in Nepal. In that case, the motivation is simple. But in our complex society, there are also other layers of needs and wants.

Research reveals that success in any area—as a business person, as a parent, as a scholar—comes from motivation. And motivation comes from a sense of satisfaction. This satisfaction comes from using your inherent skills, be they functional knowledge or personality skills, in an area that truly interests you, and in an environment that has values that match your own.

When you are intrinsically satisfied and feeling good, feeling joy—not because parents, teachers or peers tell you that you have done a good job, but because you feel you have accomplished something—you will be motivated to do it again. And if you are motivated, you will achieve. You will feel *successful.*

Motivation is the key to achieving your dreams, your goals.

Motivation Makes
The Difference Every Time

You may have the best equipment, the most up-to-date information, the most money, but you can always be out-sold, out-played, out-performed by someone with more motivation than you.

CHAPTER 7

You Can't Carry A Full Pack

On The First Day

*A*s we started out on what was to be a two-week acclimatization climb, each team member carried his own personal pack weighing about sixty pounds. Most of us found them too heavy at the start, so we took some of the stuff out of our packs and put it in a duffel bag. Three of us would fill up one bag. Then one of the porters took two duffel bags, tied them together and, with a tump line of plastic rope, headed off carrying 100-plus pounds.

Slowly, as the days went by, we were able to increase the loads in our personal packs. After six days, we could carry all our own stuff. We thanked and paid those porters who had been carrying our personal stuff and sent them home.

When you start a new level in school, a new job, become a new parent, buy a house or start a new relationship, you have to start slowly. You can't do everything at once. You don't have to be a hero on the first day.

Do what you can, comfortably at first, then stretch yourself, add more responsibilities, grow.

Life Is Not a Macho Sport

You can't do everything at once, on the first

day in a job, or the first year of a relationship.

Take on what you can carry safely and get

help with the rest. As you gain experience and

strength, you can take on extra responsibilities

and slowly increase the load you carry in life.

CHAPTER 8

Seven Asses

The first real hill we came to was a long, slow climb up, not very tall, only an 800-foot vertical drop. It was a gradual climb up. It was about the size and slope of a bunny hill at a ski resort. We started up.

Before long, I fell behind. My legs felt like rubber. I wasn't sure they would hold my weight. My breathing became faster and faster. My mouth got drier. I started second-guessing my training. Maybe I was okay in the gym, but here, in real life, I was in trouble.

I had to get a grip on myself. I went back to my training: What was the goal for today? Where were we going and when did we have to be there?

We had discussed today's plan. I knew what we hoped to do. Our goal was to reach the village at the top of the hill and stop for lunch. I didn't have to prepare the lunch, so I could get there just in time to eat at noon.

I plodded on, one step at a time, knowing I would get there eventually and that each step increased my strength, my stamina, my confidence. I had done it before. I could do it again. I knew the goal. I could do it.

When Jimmy got to the village at the top of the hill, he looked back down to see where I was. He saw, he told me later, seven asses climbing up the hill: six were donkeys carrying village supplies and the seventh was me, tagging along behind them, holding onto the last donkey's tail.

Many difficulties in our personal and professional lives come because we don't discuss our expectations. "I thought you were going to have that done today" often elicits the response, "No, I said I was going to get it done as soon as possible." Everyone has to clearly know the goal.

Set Clear Goals
and
Communicate Them Clearly

You don't have to get there first, as long as you

get there when you are supposed to. Plan all

the details, discuss all the details, review the

variations permissable, and then let individuals

use their own judgement in the execution of the

short- and long-term goals.

CHAPTER 9

The Children of Nepal

*I*n the village at the top of the hill, children gathered around to touch us and our equipment. They were dressed in rags. They just stared at us, with smiles on their faces and curiosity in their eyes.

My first reaction was to ignore them. I was too tired, and after all, we were climbing a mountain! We didn't have time to waste on kids. Then I remembered

Christine, a shy fourteen-year-old kid in the village of Whale Cove on the western shores of Hudson's Bay in the Arctic. I owned a part of a company called The Arctic Trading Company which operated out of Churchill, Manitoba. In 1984, Jimmy and a friend of his, Linc Caylor, and my younger brother, Doug, went to the Arctic to fly around the villages with Keith Rawlings, the founder of The Arctic Trading Company. Our goal was to find Inuit treasures, carvings, wall-hangings, that we could put in the catalogue of the company. Whale Cove was a town of about 300, a former whaling town that now had no industry and the people there only just survived. Most were dull-eyed and in-bred, a situation compounded by the federal government who seem to believe that if we just gave them money and supplies and sent up teachers and nurses, everything would be fine. The government people forgot about pride, self-esteem, a sense of worth! And slowly they were mentally killing these wonderful, skilled, gentle people!

Christine was the only child we saw with a sparkle in her eyes. She heard it was Jimmy's sixteenth birthday, and somewhere she found the ingredients to bake a cake in celebration. We were going to set up a trust fund to get her out of the village and get her an education, but her mother, fearful of losing her child to the unknown, refused to even consider it, and sent Christine back into their squalid home. I remembered how her eyes went dull as she closed the door. On us and on her life.

Now, far away in this Nepalese village, I was tired and we were pressing on, but I remembered Christine. We could encourage these kids. We could reward their curiosity and perhaps, just perhaps, give them a chance at a better life. It also occurred to us that since they knew more about this country than we did, they might be able to help us if we got in trouble, perhaps even save our lives. They knew the paths and could help us find our way if we were lost. They also could run like the wind and, if we needed special medical help, they could get to a village far faster than we could. So we took the time to talk to them, to show them our equipment.

Involve Others

No matter how lofty your role or your goal, take the time to encourage and answer the questions of others. You meet the same people on the way down as you meet on the way up.

CHAPTER 10

Leeches, Leeches Everywhere

e had been four days on the trail when we met four German trekkers heading back to Kathmandu. They said they had turned around because of a landslide that blocked the way; they couldn't go any further. They told us we might as well turn back too. We said we couldn't, we were training for Everest and a landslide was just part of the journey.

"What about the leeches?" they asked.

"Leeches? What do you mean?" We thought there might be a translation problem.

"Bloodsuckers," they explained. No translation problem there.

"What about bloodsuckers?" we said, knowing that back home you found a few leeches under rocks and logs in the water. What problem could they be?

Well, it turned out that in this area of Nepal, particularly in the early fall after the monsoon season, leeches were on all the leaves and branches of the bushes and trees. And, as this area was basically tropical, there were bushes everywhere. In the course of a day, you could find thirty or forty leeches on various parts of your body. They don't hurt. They're not a medical problem. But they bug you. They take your mind off your goal. You lose your focus as you think about them. They get behind your ears; in your eyes; they're in your food, and in your sleeping bag.

We were about to spend five days in "leech valley." Could we handle it? I remembered that whenever I travel with one of our kids, my wife, who knows there are going to be conflicts that could ruin the trip, always sends me away with this advice: "Before you lose your cool, stop and ask yourself— *is this going to change the world?* Is it really important? If it isn't, then forget it. You'll ruin the trip by making an issue of it."

I told this story to the team and we agreed the leeches weren't going to change the world. We'd just have to get control of them rather than let them control us. We decided that we could control the leeches by just burning them off our bodies or dousing them with salt, watching them dry up and flicking them off. And we knew we had to attempt the landslide area. So we went on.

What about the "leeches" in your life? Bosses, paperwork, teachers, traffic jams, taxes, construction on the road when you are hurrying to your next stop, nit-pickers who return your exams or application forms because of a minor problem? Leeches. Are you going to control them, or are they going to control you?

Is It Going to Change the World?

There will always be things to bug you.

Stop. Decide if the irritant is a real priority,

if it is going to change the world. If not, get

control of it, and yourself. Only worry about

the things you can change and the things

that really affect your performance.

CHAPTER 11

Crossing a Landslide — Step… by …Step

*T*n this area, the monsoon rains fall constantly throughout June, July, and August. It was September 1988, so there had been three months of monsoon rains. The hills were soaked, and every once in a while a piece of a hill would break loose and just slide away, creating a landslide. The slide that had stopped the Germans lay ahead. It was about a quarter of a mile wide. It was wet, loose clay, with rocks scattered throughout the clay. All signs of vegetation were buried under the slide. This was where I learned about team bonding.

We moved across the landslide carefully, about ten feet apart from each other. The first member put his foot out and stepped gingerly on a nearby stone or rock, pushing down to see if it was solid. When he found a solid one, he shouted "Yo" and stepped on it. Then, with his other foot, he searched for another solid rock—"Yo."

One step at a time, following the leader, attempting to step in his footsteps, we moved across the landslide. Each team member stepped out, found a secure rock and "Yo," he moved a step forward. It took us all morning to inch across the slide—a distance that would have taken less than ten minutes on a normal mountain path.

Every second our lives were in danger.

Every second our lives were in danger. If one person got sloppy, if one person didn't take the time to get a secure footing, he would slide, we would slide, and the mountain would slide. We would die. We were interdependent, co-dependent—totally. If one person slipped, we all slipped. We all died.

My mind wandered. Quickly I got control of it, but then I lost it again. I wondered what I was doing there. Then a rock got firmer and I relaxed. Just as quickly, the next one slipped under my foot. Then I reached the point of no return. I was committed. Sometimes my foot slipped just a little bit. My stomach leapt into my throat. Panic! I got control. I took my time. One step at a time.

What a stupid way to die, I thought. On a gentle slope, not even on a mountain. Death crept into my thoughts. I pushed it away. Concentrate. Take a step. How's the guy in front doing? Step. Don't think. Focus. Step. I waited for everyone to get secure and shout "Yo." My mind wandered. Grab it, bring it back. Slowly. Focus. Things became black and white. Life and death. Nothing else mattered. My body didn't hurt; I wasn't aware of breathing. Step. Step. I talked to the guy in front of me. To the guy behind me. Keep talking, keep in touch. Keep encouraging. The talk helps him and it helps me. Any phrases, anything at all, just to keep us awake, thinking, concentrating. For hours we felt our way, one step at a time.

In a family, in a relationship, in an office, in a school, everyone is interdependent. No man is an

island. There is very little you can do *all* by yourself. But to achieve the most, you have to talk, to listen, to keep in touch with everyone who has a potential impact on you.

In life you get bogged down. But do you take the time to talk to those around you? Your schedule is hectic, too hectic. You bring the pressure home. But what about your spouse's schedule? Is it only you bearing the load? Keep in touch. The family, the office, the friends. . . we are all interdependent.

We got to the other side. Safely. But we were drained, physically and mentally.

We sat down. Breathed. Relaxed. Slept.

Team Bonding

We are all interdependent. We not only have to get there ourselves, but we have to help others get there because we can't go on alone. Even if we, as individuals, do well, we may ultimately fail because we didn't help others succeed.

CHAPTER 12

In the Path of an Avalanche

*J*immy fell asleep on a rock. Another team member, Jeff, was whipped. And I was what my kids call "toast." It took two hours to recuperate from crossing the landslide. Slowly we started to drink, to eat, to get our energy and our focus back.

Eventually we talked about the crossing. Slowly jokes crept into the conversation, gentle teasing: "I thought you'd lost it." "Boy, you were slow." "Why didn't you follow my footsteps?" We relaxed, glad to be alive. We bonded. Knowing that we had each helped each other made us stronger and more confident, individually, and as a team. We were growing, physically and mentally.

And then there was a thunderclap. We looked up, but it was clear, blue sky. It wasn't thunder. It was an avalanche. About half a mile up the river from where we were still sitting, the mountain had collapsed. If we had started out five minutes earlier. . . .

Sometimes you have to be lucky. We could not have predicted the slide.

Things happen. All you can do is the best you can. We gulped back thoughts of "what if we had started out . . . ." We regrouped, refocused. We were ready. We had to be ready.

You can't plan for every eventuality. And you can't let the unexpected stop you. You absorb, you make the necessary changes, but you go on.

We went on, through what I call Bali Hai. Dense, beautiful forests, with huge red rhododendrons and sparkling streams. Ravines and gorges, one hundred

feet across with swinging bridges that are centuries
old. These, in fact, are not only beautiful, but they
build confidence and foster teamwork. You can't go
across as a team unless you develop a rhythm because
the bridge undulates and you have to be in sync.

The rivers cascade over the chasms, tumbling two,
three, four thousand feet down. Falls, ten, twenty,
thirty feet across, fall thousands of feet. Spectacular,
but with our focus on the job at hand, we often didn't
recognize the beauty until we saw the pictures later!

On and on we continued through Leech Valley.

But now we were in control. They didn't bug us.

Sometimes You Have to be Lucky

But, as has been said, the more you practise,

the luckier you get.

CHAPTER 13

The Corn Woman

*W*e were starting to feel confident, capable. We could carry seventy- to eighty-pound packs now. We were climbing steeper and steeper valleys, pushing ourselves harder and harder. We weren't feeling the weight of our packs as much and our breathing wasn't as laboured. Even as we went through the 11,000-foot level, where the oxygen content of the air begins its exponential decline, our cardiovascular systems kept getting stronger and we could suck in greater quantities of air and thus get the required oxygen. Our confidence in ourselves and in the team grew. We even got feeling cocky. We were getting ready for the big mountain—Everest.

And then she came along. A woman carrying about one hundred pounds of corn on her back. She was about five feet tall and couldn't have weighed more than 100 pounds herself! She lived in one of the little villages perched on the side of the steep valleys. Each village might house three or four families and assorted goats, chickens, and dogs. Often, the only flat plateaus to grow any crops were five or six miles away, up and down the valleys. So the people of the village would plant corn and other crops, and when it was time to harvest, the women would walk to the plateau, cut the corn at ground level (saving the stalks and all) and then, one by one, they would bend over while others piled the corn stalks and ears on their backs. When the weight was such that they could hardly stand up, a rope was tied around the corn and they would slowly, carefully, trudge up and down the

And then she came along.

A woman carrying about

one hundred pounds of

corn on her back.

valleys, back to the village. Often it would take a couple of days to get home.

Watching this woman put our loads, our tasks, in perspective.

Keeping Perspective

Sometimes we think we are carrying all the

troubles of the earth. But others carry loads

too.

CHAPTER 14

How Far
Is Too Far?

*W*e spent the next four days going up and down the sides of the valley—sometimes on horizontal paths, sometimes on verticals with no paths.

Up and down.

We would go up 600 feet, pushing ourselves as hard as we could. And then, when we were just at our limit, when we could hardly breathe, we would come back down 100 feet. Up 800 feet, down 100 feet. Up 1,600 feet, down 200 feet. Now we were pushing ourselves hard, getting ready for Everest. We were doing three things:

1. Pushing our cardiovascular systems as hard as we could to increase our oxygen-absorbing capacity.
2. Pushing our legs and upper bodies, extending them each step, trying to increase our physical strength.
3. Building the team. As we pushed, we learned more about each other. Slowly our roles in the team developed: the ones who were always out front pushing themselves and pulling the rest of us; the ones who were slower and needed encouragement; the ones who brought a sense of humour that kept us going; the ones measuring our capacity, when we had gone too far, too hard and needed to slow down or go down; and the administrators, those who kept track of our food and drink requirements as

well as organizing the set-up and breakdown of camp.

We were becoming a team, confident and cognizant of ourselves and the others. We pushed ourselves as hard as we could, then eased off a bit; pushed again, then eased off, pushed, then eased off.

No one can go full tilt all the time. We all need to ease back physically and mentally every once in a while. If we don't, we get sloppy, we lose concentration, we slip, fall, die.

I was beginning to understand why we were doing this acclimatization climb. I was overwhelmed at how little I knew about my mind, and my body. I made comparisons to jobs I'd had, to schoolwork.

At home we sometimes keep pressing on. "I'll pull another all-nighter to get this essay done."

"I know it's late and I'm tired, but if I just drive the last 200 miles, I'll be home for the weekend."

"We need that presentation for tomorrow at 8:00 a.m. Keep going until you get it done. I know this is the third one this week, but the client wants it." Full tilt. . . but not all the time. Balance is necessary. We have to understand our own capacity.

I remember in my scuba training that they said when you know you are out of air, when your lungs are bursting, that you can still live another two minutes. So I know, even when I think I have nothing left to give, there is probably a little more inside. But I also know that just as I can stretch an elastic too far and it will break, so can I try to do too much and I will physically or mentally break. How far is too far? In physical black and white activities like climbing, it becomes easier to judge. You begin to sense your mind wandering or your feet slipping, not landing on exactly the spot on the ledge that you aimed for. You have to be incredibly sensitive to these nuances and recognize them for what they are: you are at your limit; slow down, go down. The balance comes because you want to go as far as you can, to stay with the team, but you don't want to get sloppy. When one person reaches his limit, the whole team stops and goes down. The pressure to keep going is constant, not to be the first to say "I have to stop," not to be the one to hold the team back. You have to stretch and grow, but not break.

At home, in the job, at school, this line is harder to recognize because there are so many components to your life. But if you recognize the principle of "stretch and grow, but not break," if you utilize this principle and the ones discussed later in this book as a template to judge your activities, you begin to make better decisions.

You have to stretch and grow, but not break.

You Can't Go Full Tilt All the Time

*If you don't have a change of pace, you will
perish. You have to take holidays, do physical
activities. The job is important and there are
things you have to get done. But few, if any,
of us can go full-tilt all the time in the job
without paying a terrible price in health, in
family, in personal relationships.*

CHAPTER 15

Sometimes You Lead,
Sometimes You Follow

arry had spent a lot of time choosing the members of his team. He knew from experience how important the skills were, but he also knew how the intangibles like chemistry, attitude, and motivation were. He knew very well the impact these latter factors could have on the success or failure of the climb. In 1982, sixteen of Canada's top climbers went to Everest. Two Canadians and three Sherpas got to the top—success—but four died; there were three changes in leadership before the climb even started; over half the team quit because of a difference in values. It wasn't a team; it was a group of All-Stars, each wanting to run his own little climb, irrespective of the needs of the team.

To build a team, you need more than a goal. You need a strategy that everyone understands and believes in. You need definition of roles that are agreed to; it is unlikely that everyone will make it to the top, so are there role players who will willingly break the trail, set the ropes?

You need communication throughout the climb, because things change and people have to know the impact of these changes. If a route change is necessary because of an avalanche and more technical skills are needed for the new route, will everyone agree to the new route and the new roles for people?

Finally, you need commitment, commitment to the goal of the team getting to the top, not any individual in particular, but the team. It is not enough to tell people to act like a team; they need to experience it. That was a key reason for the acclimatization climb; it would be too late to learn this on Everest.

When I first got involved with Outward Bound, the leading organization in the world in the field of experiential education, I soon discovered that true learning is the result of actually *doing* something as opposed to being *told* about it or being told that you could do it. The same lesson applied to Everest Express; we needed to work together as a team in order to become a team. I also realized that although I was usually in a leadership role at home, over here I could, and had to, follow others. They knew more than I did, were more capable mountain climbers than I was and, as I gained respect for them, I could easily follow them. But I also realized that I had something to offer: my age, my variety of experience, and my perspective on life gave me some insight into situations that could help them. We each had something to offer and we began to recognize the value of each of us.

Sometimes you lead and sometimes you follow. There may not be anyone who can lead all the people, all the time. One night about five days into the climb, after several setbacks with the porters, the route, the weather (it was always raining!), we started to bitch. Everyone vented his pet peeves and the session turned a bit ugly. Interestingly, it was Jimmy, the youngest member of the team, who

We needed to work together as a team in order to become a team.

stopped us by reminding us that this acclimatization climb was organized to work out just the details we were bitching about, so what was the problem? He brought us back to reality and the task at hand.

Everyone has a role. You have to find it, believe in it and use it. And you have to communicate, and talk out problems so they don't become crises.

The roles were being defined. Our strength—muscular, cardiovascular, and mental—was increasing exponentially; and we were becoming a capable and effective team.

Everyone Has A Role

Everyone has a role, but it must be both accepted and comfortable to the individual and the team. And roles often change based on the circumstances at hand. The key is to discover what you and the others do best, and maximize those skills at the appropriate opportunities.

![Chapter icon]

CHAPTER 16

Jimmy's Life at Stake

*O*ne of the results of the summer monsoons was the creation of rivers and waterfalls as the water tumbled off the mountain tops. On the seventh day of the acclimatization climb, I counted eighty-nine rivers, some two feet wide, some twenty feet wide.

One river is particularly memorable to me. It was about fifteen feet wide, in yet another valley, surrounded by lush vegetation and, at first glance, just another river pouring off the mountain and over a cliff into the valley. Jimmy was the first to cross. Halfway across, he stepped on a rock, pushed off, and the rock slipped.

Without the support of the rock, he fell into the river. Although it was only a couple of feet deep, the power of the rushing water carried him downstream about ten feet. He tumbled and twisted, trying to catch on to a rock to arrest his slide, trying to get his feet in front of him to brace himself and stop his downward rush. Then he suddenly stopped. A rock, about eighteen inches high, had caught between his pack and his bum, bringing him to an abrupt halt in the swirling river. He had stopped about four feet from the top of a waterfall that fell 1,000 feet to the valley below.

He hung there, the rock holding him back from the edge of the cliff.

My first reaction was to shout, "Look out! Hold on! Be careful!" But something stopped me. Those words not only wouldn't help, they would probably confuse him.

I couldn't help him. If I started toward him, I might dislodge another rock, I might change the direction or pressure of the water and he might slip off the rock that was holding him above the waterfall. I had to stand, twenty feet from my son, and watch him hang at the edge of a 1,000-foot cliff, *and I couldn't do a thing to help him.*

I stood there. Options raced through my mind. I was unable to evaluate them. Everything seemed right, and everything seemed impossible.

He could die. I had to do something. But what? I was transfixed. No one moved. We were afraid that any movement in the river might dislodge him. I kept waiting for someone to take control, for someone, anyone, to do something.

We couldn't do anything. We didn't have enough information and we couldn't get it. My son was near the edge of a cliff. One wrong move and he would fall to his death. And I couldn't do anything.

When our kids are having trouble with relationships; when our friends are making decisions about buying a bigger house or adding to their mortgage to take a vacation; when a peer decides to take on the boss in a no-win situation; sometimes we have to leave them alone, not get involved, not put in our two-cents worth.

I kept waiting

for someone to take

control, for someone,

anyone, to do something.

Sometimes You Have to Leave Them Alone

You may be the parent, the boss, or the teacher, but there will be times when you can't do anything without increasing the risk. Sometimes you have to leave them alone.

CHAPTER 17

Our Only Chance to Save Jimmy

*J*immy slowly reached back, looking for a secure handhold. His hand found only loose rocks, nothing that could support his weight. Then finally he reached to his left and found some rocks that didn't shift when he grasped them. He would be able to put his weight on them. Now he needed a way back upstream.

"Throw me a rope," he called over his shoulder.

I grabbed one and was about to throw it when I realized I was probably the least competent rope-thrower in our group. I handed the rope to Dixon.

"But he's my son!" I pleaded. "Be careful."

Dixon leaned back and threw. The rope landed right over Jimmy's shoulder. He tied it around his chest and we pulled him back up the river.

When he was close to shore, I waded out and grabbed him. I cried, quietly at first and then giant sobs. My mind whirled. What if the rope toss hadn't reached him? What if, what if...? I struggled to gain control, to give him someone to lean on, something solid. But I couldn't.

Eventually we both recovered from the ordeal—he was the first, despite the physical and emotional toll the experience had taken. When I had time to collect my thoughts, I realized there are lots of other situations in which it's smarter to take advice or instruction from a colleague. It's often tough to talk to our kids. A close friend might be more effective than us at giving advice about what to wear for that job interview. You may be the boss, but a peer may be more effective in telling one of your staff that his sarcasm is wearing thin. Sometimes another person is better at the job—as Dixon was. Sometimes it is best to let somebody else do it.

Sometimes You Have to Let Somebody Else Do It

Even though you're the boss, or the parent,

someone else may be more capable. Don't try

to be a hero. Let the most competent person

do what has to be done.

CHAPTER 18

Another Hundred Pounds of Corn

*I*t took Jimmy about fifteen minutes to settle down; he fiddled with his belt, his camera, his pack. We waited.

Finally he said, "Let's go."

As we walked away, I savoured him with my eyes. I couldn't let him out of my sight.

And then she came along. Another woman from another village, carrying about 100 pounds of corn, slowly moving it from the field to her family.

She didn't care about my problems . . . and I didn't give a damn about hers.

A reminder that life goes on and others have loads to carry too.

Everyone Has a Load to Carry

Remember, you aren't the only one with cares

or concerns. We all get tied up in ourselves and

forget about others. They have problems too.

Some people carry enormous loads.

CHAPTER 19

The Challenges In Front of Us

The next morning we came to the base of a steep climb. We stopped for something to eat and drink and I caught Dixon looking back. A 400-foot cliff stood in front of us, and he was looking

back. I reminded him about looking ahead, about goal setting, visioning.

"That's how you achieve great things," I told him. "That's how you climb that cliff."

He said he was just looking back at where we'd been.

"No," I exhorted."Look ahead. Envision yourself climbing that cliff."

Quietly, he suggested that we could learn a lot by looking back at where we had been.

"What do you mean?" I asked.

"Look back at what we have already climbed," he said. "Don't those accomplishments give you confidence for the challenges in front of us?"

He reminded me that we often belittle what we've done, whereas we should remember how tough the challenge seemed at the time. We should give ourselves credit for our past accomplishments. The future challenges wouldn't necessarily be the same as the past, but what we had done in the past should give us confidence to face the future.

We should give

ourselves credit for

past accomplishments.

He was right. I'd gotten so caught up in the challenges ahead and in goal setting that I hadn't given myself credit for what I'd already climbed. (Thanks, Dixon.)

This lesson applies to lots of things. Remember when you first entered high school? It was terrifying, you couldn't get over the size of the place. When you left high school, you knew the place and the people backwards and forwards, but college was really terrifying! When you left college, you understood it, but starting a job! We have to stop and give ourselves credit for our accomplishments as we go along.

You Can Learn a Lot by Looking Back

Take a moment to look back, to reflect on previous accomplishments, and use them as a basis for building confidence as you accept future challenges.

CHAPTER 20

Climbing in the Clouds

After eight days we reached the little village of Kuldi Gar, where we overnighted. As we set out the next morning, I noticed that Jimmy seemed to be unsteady on his feet. I caught up to him and quickly saw that he was glassy-eyed and feverish. We went to the village and Dr. Carl put him to bed with a fever of 104°F. It was obvious that we were going to be here for a day or two, so we relaxed.

Some rested, some chatted, I shuttled in and out of Jimmy's little cabin. As I sat at his door, looking down the valley, I noticed the clouds moving in and out of the valley. In four minutes the weather could change in the valley from a clear view to one filled with clouds. As I watched the clouds, I naturally wondered about their impact on our climb. You become very sensitive to everything around you, always relating it to your activities, your goals, your strategies. I realized that for a mountain climber, these clouds were treacherous. Inside a cloud you can't see, and everything you grab is slippery.

I immediately began to evaluate the consequences. What do you do, as a climber, when the clouds come in? It was obvious we were going to be staying put for a couple of days, but what if we met the same situation after we started moving again?

I should review the options so I'd be prepared for the future. It seemed to me that we could hang on and wait until the clouds disappeared. But that could be two minutes or a couple of days. If we were in the

In four minutes

the weather could change

in the valley from a clear

view to one filled with clouds.

middle of a climb and the clouds came in, we could go back down to get out of them, back to a more secure footing or handhold, but going down is as tough as going up. So, I concluded, I guess you would keep going up. Slowly.

Instead of a fully extended reach up, you just reach up a foot or so, slowly, cautiously, never losing your grip. As soon as you find a new handhold, you feel around it to be sure it is secure, solid, and then you slowly dry it off with your hands.

Then you hang on, and with your other hand you find another hold, dry it, hang on. Then you move one foot, then the other foot. Slowly, carefully, always keeping three holds secure, you move up through the clouds.

In life, we often don't know what to do, which way to go. We can't see an obvious next step. The way is cloudy. Inexperience, changing laws, complications, inhibit our decision-making skills.

What do you do? Quit, leave, do nothing? No. You search for the familiar, the secure, the obvious and move ahead slowly, carefully.

Jimmy got better. In two days the fever broke and we went on.

When You Don't Know What to Do, Do It Slowly

Times change, jobs change, rules change. So what do you do? Throw up your hands? Quit? No. If you don't know what to do next, if the next step is unclear, go to the things you know. Rebuild the scenario. Look for things you might have missed. Move ahead slowly. Take small steps, and complete them one at a time. The fastest way to do it is to do it slowly.

CHAPTER 21

Sleeping on a 3,000-Foot Vertical

*W*hen I think I just can't do something, I can't go any farther, I remember the next three days. We stood on a hill, looking down one side of a cliff and up the other side. We had about a 1,000-foot climb down and then had to go up the other side—about 3,000 feet of vertical rock that reached far above our heads. It seemed impossible to me even with all that we had done so far. The challenges just seemed to get bigger and bigger. And we hadn't even started Everest yet!

I wondered if I could do it. My inspiration came from the stories of other climbs and other climbers. Stories of climbers sleeping on vertical cliffs.

How do you sleep on a vertical? Climbers, with their ingenuity and determination, have developed a wall-sleeping system that relies on pitons—the spike-like metal pieces they drive into the rock to give them support. I can assure you that you spend a lot of time pounding those pitons in, making sure they are secure. If they aren't and they slip, you die.

In our lives, we have pitons. They are our support systems: knowledge, technology, people. Do we take the time to be sure we are secure? Do we update our technical skills frequently? Do we read and keep up-to-date on information relating to our jobs?

And how about people? "Oh, I worked with her ten years ago. Haven't talked to her since, but I'm sure she'll help." Not necessarily! We need to keep in touch with friends, spouses, parents, kids, and career

The challenges just

seemed to get bigger

and bigger.

associates. They may have developed other lives and allegiances and we may be cut out.

On the mountain, if your pitons are not secure, you fall and die. Back here, you don't die, but you may fall.

I went on, remembering those other climbers, their ingenuity and strength—mental and physical.

It Is Amazing What You Can Do

There is hardly anything you can't do if you have, and you nurture, the proper support systems. Don't lower the goal, increase your support.

CHAPTER 22

Cerebral Edema
Strikes Two of Our Climbers

*W*e finally got to Base Camp in the Annapurna Range, 13,000 feet up the mountain, among glaciers and moraines. There was still about 4,000 feet of mountain in front of us, but our plan was to settle here and go out for a day at a time and play on the glaciers, on the rocks, just to practise and push ourselves at this new altitude. In fact, this is a camp that trekkers, using a walking trail, often come to. There is a stone "lodge" here, with about 20 rough bunkbeds and a cookhouse.

We set up camp. The first night, two of our team members, Jeff and Gary, didn't sleep well. They had headaches, which are the first sign of altitude sickness, of cerebral edema—the first thing that Barry told Jimmy could kill you on the mountain. They were also confused, disoriented. In severe cases, they could lose consciousness. The only cure is to get down, fast, to where there is more oxygen and more air pressure.

They talked to Carl, our doctor. He confirmed that they had cerebral edema. They discussed it and decided they wanted to go down and out, leave the team, and not go on to Everest.

The rest of us decided to go back out with them, back to Kathmandu. It didn't take a long time to reach this conclusion. We were worried about them, and we had built up such a strong team that we knew there was no choice. And, ultimately, we had already achieved the most important goals of this part of the climb: acclimatization and team-building.

The Laws of Nature Cannot Be Violated

When there is no choice, do what is necessary.

And then get on with it.

CHAPTER 23

I Push Myself Too Far

As we were packing to leave, I approached Jimmy.

"When we get back to Kathmandu and Gary and Jeff head back to Canada, should we go back home with them? You've already had a rough time, what with hanging over that cliff and running a temperature of 104°F? And Everest will only be tougher. What do you think?"

"You've had a rough time too, Dad," he pointed out.

And I had. We had been trekking for fourteen hours a day, for each of the last three days. I was whipped by the time the third day started. Part way up the last day's climb, it was obvious I was having trouble. On a ledge, the others took some stuff out of my pack to lighten my load. Dixon found a paperback book in my pack. He was astounded. I lamely said that I might want to relax by reading, that it was inspirational. He tossed it off the cliff. Fortunately he didn't find the little kids' book that a friend, Mandy, had given me, *The Little Engine That Could*—it *was* inspirational.

Finally, they took my pack from me and Archie and Hank talked me up the last 200 feet. Although Hank was a big bull of a man, he was also a gentle nurturer who not only recognized the signs of sheer burnout, but could help. Archie was a slight, gentle man, with an unflagging willingness and capacity to do whatever had to be done to help the team or an individual.

At the top, I sagged to the ground unable to hold myself up and hardly able to breathe. Carl saw I was in trouble and came over. He noticed I was having difficulty swallowing. I was dehydrated — almost totally dehydrated. Carl told me that without the slow re-introduction of water into my system, I could die. He dipped his finger in a cup of water and touched it to my tongue. One drop at a time, he re-hydrated me. I couldn't absorb any more than a drop at a time. I was like parched soil in the desert that the water runs off.

I was out of balance. I had worked so hard at The Fitness Institute to discipline my mind, to keep going when my body screamed in pain, to keep going mentally, because I knew that my old body wouldn't be able to keep up with the younger climbers. I knew I had to be stronger mentally in order to keep going and survive.

And I was mentally strong, too strong. I did not have the balance between my mind and my body. We need balance between health, job, family, friends, leisure. And when we get out of balance, we risk collapsing; we risk failure. I have a friend named Pat who says there are four legs to her stool: family, personal growth, friends, and career. And she knows when she is out of balance because her weight balloons.

Balance is not necessarily 25%, 25%, 25%, 25%. It is whatever you think is right for you. It means no regrets, no "I should be. . ." in our lives. But it is definitive, not a loose guess that we modify as we go along.

Finally, I could swallow a cup of water, but I was exhausted. I fell asleep without eating. The next day, I

When we get out of balance,

we risk collapsing; we risk

failure.

started out with Hank before the rest of the team because I knew I would have trouble maintaining their pace.

Jimmy was right. I had had a rough time too.

"Do you want to go home?" he asked.

"You want to go on, don't you?" I replied.

"Yes," he said emphatically. "We came over here to go to Everest, so let's go to Everest."

We trekked back to Pokhara and took a plane to Kathmandu. There, we spent a day in the luxury of a hotel, with beds, showers, and cooked meals!

After relaxing, re-equipping ourselves as necessary, and seeing Jeff and Gary off to Canada, we boarded a plane to Lhasa, in Tibet.

Our sights were now set on Everest. The Tibetans call it Chomolungma, The Mother Goddess of the World.

Balance

A one-legged stool will never stand.

You need several legs to support a life —
health, career, family, personal growth,
friends ... the list can be long. Decide what's
important to you and what proportion of
your life you'll devote to each element. Time
will change the proportions, but if you don't
establish and articulate your priorities,
you'll always be unhappy, second-guessing
yourself, regretfull ... out of balance.

CHAPTER 24

Now We Are a Real Team

*D*uring tryouts, even when the team was finally chosen and we shared activities such as preparing food lists and getting the equipment organized, we didn't really know each other. Now we did. Now we trusted and respected each other. And whereas at the start of the climb, I could introduce them only by name, now I can introduce them with some substance and affection.

Barry Blanchard

Marc Twight

Barry Blanchard was the Expedition Leader. His climbing partner was Marc Twight. They were and are professional climbers. They lived to climb. They came down off a mountain only long enough to organize their next climb. They were totally focused on the goal: the summit of Everest. But they knew they needed a support team to help them reach that goal. Barry chose carefully.

Carl Hannigan

Carl Hannigan was our mountain doctor. A veterinarian by training, but a trained mountaineering medic. He was a bull of a man, whose legs and heart just kept churning at the same pace no matter how steep the incline or how long the day. This strength belied his sensitivity and awareness of us and our individual physical needs. He watched and helped in a preventive sense as well as remedial.

Chris Considine

Chris Considine was a lawyer, a powerful courtroom orator and thinker, whose lean physique had been honed by years of trekking and climbing. The outdoors was his refuge from the life-and-death pressures of the courtroom. He was engaged to be married soon after our return. He climbed steadily, but always seemed to sense when others needed help or an issue needed defusing.

John Morel was a cabinet-maker and jewellry maker, a master craftsman. He was slight of build but physically and mentally the toughest, most determined, most willing man I have ever met. He always offered to carry the extra load, to go ahead, go back, do whatever needed to be done. A workhorse with a smile and a self-deprecating demeanour.

John Morel

Archie Louis was a second-generation Chinese Canadian. This caused the Tibetans some confusion: Archie spoke only English, and they couldn't understand why he could not talk with them even though he looked like them. He was single, in his early thirties. He designed our team logo. If he sensed something needed to be done, he grabbed it and did it. No fuss, no discussion, just do it and get on.

Archie Louis

Hank Van Weelden, like Carl, had the build of a Mack truck. He also had an enquiring mind and a subtle sense of humour that prodded us on and made us smile. Time and time again, he fell back to talk with me, gently urging me on and building my confidence. He was single, a veteran climber.

Hank Van Weelden

Jim Law, an account supervisor at Hayhurst Communications in Calgary, was in his early thirties, married with two children. His willingness to just keep climbing resulted in things getting done. He learned quickly and then would set the pace to ensure that we got where we wanted to go.

Jim Law

Ric Singleton

Ric Singleton, like me, was in his forties. He was an architect, married with no children. He brought great balance to the team. His physical strength and curiosity kept us going and trying new things when we should have been tired and dispirited.

Tom Christie

Tom Christie was a stockbroker, single, in his late twenties. His determination resulted in him carrying more than his share of the load; he just kept going.

Dixon Thompson

Dixon Thompson, a professor, was the other elder statesman of the group. He was an experienced mountain expedition leader, had a wealth of experience, and a maturity that helped all of us keep perspective. His insight into situations, both on the mountain and in the group dynamics, was vital to our team building.

Jeff Goguen

Jeff Goguen was single, in his late twenties, and a venture capital accountant. He hoped to buy a business on his return. He had the strength and mental toughness to do anything. Were it not for the cerebral edema that forced him to turn back at Annapurna Base Camp, he would have been a driving force on the team at Everest.

Gary Gault

Gary Gault was in his early thirties, single, and had his own accounting practice, specializing in oil and gas. He brought balance to all that we did. Physical strength and a sense of balance in his life made him a major asset. He would have been a major contributor at Everest had he not been forced to stop climbing because of cerebral edema.

Jimmy

Jimmy's youthful exuberance, physical strength, and basic honesty added enormously to the trip. He savoured the climbing, the new experiences, and plunged into the inevitable politics of a group with a refreshing innocence that charmed us out of our infighting.

I think I brought a sense of humour and a base of experience from Outward Bound that added depth to our physical exertions. Physically, I was at the tail of the team, but mentally, I hope, I added to the growth of each of us.

You Have to Live and Work Together to Really Know Each Other

In a real team — an effective, successful team — everyone knows and trusts each other. This intimacy comes only with time and shared experiences.

CHAPTER 25

Everest

*E*verest. The tallest mountain in the world: 29,028 feet or 8,848 metres high.

So tall it creates its own weather system.

Strikingly beautiful, far above pollution, where the sky is a deep blue and the snow a vivid white.

But Everest is also vicious, with temperatures of -60°F, winds up to 150 miles per hour and two feet of snow in an hour. And it can snow for 12 hours!

And huge! We travelled from Lhasa by Toyota Land Cruiser for three days, winding our way to and up the mountain. Past Tibetan monasteries, up, up the mountain range, working our way deeper and deeper into the Himalayas.

And then suddenly we came around the corner of another mountain and there, right in front of us, was Everest, sparkling in the noonday sun. And then, just as fast, it was gone, shrouded in clouds.

We could see the summit of Everest from Base Camp when the clouds receded. We could also see that even though we were at 17,000 feet above sea level, we were only two-thirds of the way up the mountain, and still six horizontal miles from the peak. This is a huge mountain!

Our two tons of supplies had been delivered to Base Camp at Everest, and Barry and Marc were there when we arrived. They'd gone ahead to start acclimatizing.

The rest of us settled into Base Camp, adjusting to the new altitude. We were well acclimatized to life at 13,000 feet—the altitude at Base Camp in the Annapurna Range and at Lhasa. But from now on the decrease in air pressure and oxygen would be exponential. Everest Base Camp, at 17,000 feet, had only 70% of the oxygen per cubic foot that Lhasa had at 13,000 feet, and about half the oxygen found at sea level.

Base Camp was set up in a rocky moraine. A moraine is formed from debris left by a glacier as it recedes. It was flat, about one-half mile wide, with no vegetation. Big and small rocks, boulders, no animal life, a bleak, barren wasteland.

The camp consisted of a cook tent, a mountain of supplies, and seven of our two-man tents. The two primary climbers, Barry and Marc, and the primary support team, John and Hank, would consider this home for the next five weeks. The rest of us, the secondary support team, would be here only long enough to acclimatize and then help move supplies up the mountain to the Advance Camp in the 21,000-foot area. We expected to be there a little over a week and then to go back to Lhasa.

The goal of our climb was to give our two primary climbers, Barry Blanchard and Marc Twight, a crack at the peak. There could be no questions about that

There could be no

questions about that goal—

everyone had to understand

and commit to it.

goal—everyone had to understand and commit to it. However, the strategies to accomplish it might change at any time. We spent our first two days at Base Camp discussing our goal, the plan, the options, the strategies. We planned to do an Alpine-style climb. That meant we would carry our own stuff, no Sherpas as mountain guides, and no porters. (The other climbing style is Assault, where Sherpas, porters, and climbers leap-frog camps up the mountain. It takes more people, more money, more equipment, and more organization.) In order to give Barry and Marc a chance to reach the top, the rest of us acted basically as porters ferrying stuff up the mountain.

In real life, several of us ran our own businesses, others were managers. Yet on this climb, we were porters, taking orders, carrying back-breaking loads, with no chance of having a crack at the peak and little chance of being the focus of the glory. We were commited to the process.

When Barry built the team, he made sure that we understood, accepted, and were enthusiastic about our roles. He didn't want our egos getting in the way of the real objective. That's why, before he signed us up, he needed to know our attitudes and our values, as well as our technical capabilities. That's why the try-outs in Montana and the acclimatization climb at Annapurna were so important: to help each of us understand our capacity and our roles.

Expeditions often fail to reach the top because the climbers hold back, saving their strength, so that when the time come to choose the final assault team, they will be in the best shape. The problem is, without their help in the grunt work, no one gets a chance at the peak.

I've been told that more have died on Everest than have reached the summit. And more have died on the way down than on the way up. Sometimes people get sloppy, sometimes they fall off the side, sometimes slides kill them, sometimes the edema kills them. On the way down, without the goal of the peak, the adrenalin slows down and people lose their focus, and they die.

Define Roles and Goals

Shared goals and understood roles — the keys to success. If you don't know where you are going, any road will take you there. And if you don't know what you are doing, you'll never get it done.

CHAPTER 26

The Thrill of Being There —
At Base Camp

I had forgotten the

lessons I had so painfully

learned over the last

couple of weeks.

My mind boggled. We were on Everest! I was on Everest. No matter what happened now, I was on a mountain very few people in the world will ever touch. I thought of the people I had talked to, the climbers in England, Europe, and North America, who hoped, one day, to go to Everest. And here I was! I forgot about the training. I forgot about Annapurna. I forgot the fear, the hurt, the danger. I thought, "Let's get going. We're here, let's climb." I was thrilled to be there and already I had forgotten the lessons I had so painfully learned over the last couple of weeks. I was ready to forget our plan to spend a few days at Base Camp, testing loads, working out on the rocks and ice, acclimatizing at 17,000 feet. Let's get going!

But the increased altitude and decreased oxygen level were debilitating. I went to the spring to get a bucket of water the first afternoon. When I had filled it, I started back the one hundred yards to our camp. After fifty yards I had to rest. Five minutes later, I picked up the bucket and continued my haul. Twenty yards later, I sat down. I couldn't carry the bucket any farther. I crawled back to camp without the water. Four days later, after acclimatizing, I could carry two buckets the whole one hundred yards!

I settled down, partly because I ran out of energy due to the altitude and partly because my brain clicked in with lessons from the past. Key phrases such as, "you not only have to get there, you have to get back too," put me back on track.

Don't Get Cocky— Don't Forget the Lessons Learned

When you try to go too fast in school, in your job, or in relationships, you won't be ready for, or capable of adjusting to, surprises and changes. And you'll fail. Go slowly, acclimatize.

CHAPTER 27

Death at 17,000 Feet

here were two other teams on the north side with us that fall: an American team called the Cowboys who were celebrating the centennial of Wyoming, and a French team sponsored by Honeywell Bull, who were attempting to climb the Seven Peaks of the world. Both groups had arrived a couple of weeks before us.

On the third day at Base Camp, Benoît Chamoux, the leader of the French team, came over to our camp. One of his climbers, Pierre, had died of cerebral edema shortly after his arrival at Base Camp. Benoît was still grappling with the death.

We were all devastated by the news, and Benoît was, understandably, especially distraught. What could he have done? What should he have done? What should he do now? Realizing that he needed to talk, I suggested that we go for a walk. I prodded him with questions, just to keep him talking, to give him an outlet. I asked him about Pierre and about what had happened.

"He was the best. A superb climber and very unselfish. He stayed behind in Paris for a week doing public relations work for the team while the rest of us came to Everest. Then he flew to Lhasa and hurried up the mountain to meet us. Along the way he got a headache."

"That can be a sign of cerebral edema," I ventured.

"Yes, but he reasoned that he was only going up 4,000 feet: from 13,000 feet at Lhasa to 17,000 feet at Base Camp. And he knew he had easily climbed 4,000

What could he have done?

What should he have done?

What should he do now?

feet before without incident, so he decided to take some painkillers and keep going, planning to rest at Base Camp. But twenty-four hours after getting to Base Camp, the inside of his head imploded down his spinal chord and he died a vicious, writhing death." Benoît continued to talk until he wound down.

Eventually he looked at me. I tried to find some way to offer my understanding, my sympathy. I searched for words, for the right words, for anything to help him with his pain. This was all new to me and I struggled.

Slowly a metaphor formed in my mind as Benoît talked.

"Perhaps Pierre was not on The Right Mountain," I suggested.

"What do you mean?" he asked.

"I'm not sure, but I get the feeling that if Pierre had really understood himself, if he really knew how he operated and had compared that style, the things that made him so successful in Europe, with the requirements of this much different mountain, he would have realized that his normal style wouldn't work. Everest was not the right mountain for his natural behaviour."

I went on: "Pierre's natural style had been to test what he was about to do with what he had done before. If it had worked in the past, it could work now. But what he forgot was that in the past when he climbed 4,000 feet, it was from 7,000 to 11,000 feet. There is little change in air pressure or oxygen level.

"Perhaps Pierre was not

on The Right Mountain."

Now he was going 13,000 to 17,000 with the inherent huge reduction in oxygen. He needed to go slowly this time, to acclimatize.

"His experience in Europe was not transferable to Everest. He was not on The Right Mountain for his way of operating, for his skills. If he had looked at himself and at the needs of the mountain, he would have either modified his behaviour or stayed off the mountain. He either didn't understand himself or didn't compare himself with the needs of Everest. And it cost him his life."

Benoît nodded slowly. Then he thanked me. He returned to his camp, and promised to think about what I had suggested.

After he left, I thought about it too. Was I right? Was the explanation useful or was I just chattering to fill in the gaps in Benoît's search?

The enormity of my realization hit me. It made sense. Knowing who you are, knowing how you operate, your skills, and comparing them with the challenge at hand can save your life. A natural athlete can be a star in high school football, but if he wants to play in the NFL he needs to modify his behaviour: weight training, diet, drinking habits. As you get older, you can't just go on to the tennis courts without stretching exercises or pick up a trombone without regular breathing exercises. You have to change and watch your diet. You have to *modify your behaviour* in recognition of the new conditions.

Pierre should have compared his operating style with the needs of Everest. And if he saw that there wasn't a match, he should have modified his behaviour or stayed off the mountain. He didn't think of making the comparison, he just kept climbing through the pain.

Back home, in our families, in our jobs, in our relationships, we should look to see if there is a match between our values and what we are doing. And if there isn't a match, we should consider either modifying our behaviour or changing what we are doing. Now, back home, we won't die, but we will become unhappy and unsatisfied; and if we are unsatisfied, we will be unmotivated. And if we are not motivated, we will be unsuccessful. And if we are not successful, we'll probably be fired or divorced or. . . .

So it seems to be just as important here, as on the mountain, to figure out your core skills and operate consistently with them.

Know Yourself

What you have done, accomplished in the past, may not be directly applicable to the challenge of today. Knowing yourself, and comparing these skills with the challenge ahead, can enable you to adapt or adjust. Or, perhaps, stay off the mountain.

CHAPTER 28

Ric Gets Pulmonary Edema

*P*ierre's death hit us all hard. It showed us exactly what we were risking. For hours we just sat and stared at the mountain. What should we do? Had we lost our motivation? Or was it just overshadowed by the death? The thrill was gone. The death was very real.

When I began my research into this climb, I read every book on the subject and I talked to everyone I could who knew about Everest. I watched videos.

I listened to tapes. Intellectually I understood what could happen. I read about death. I understood, intellectually, that death happens.

Viscerally I had no idea. One moment Pierre was alive, the next, he was dead. Dead. Never to talk, hike, climb again.

It took two days to absorb the death and its implications. Then slowly we re-energized. Could we continue the climb? Should we? Was this death an omen? We talked. We stared at the mountain. Finally, we decided to continue and once again we set about testing our packs and building our physical and mental systems.

Then Mother Nature hit again. One morning, Ric woke up very short of breath. His lips were blue, indicating insufficient oxygen in the blood. As he inhaled, he gurgled, and as he gurgled, he was drowning. There was fluid in his lungs. He had pulmonary edema. His lungs were filling with fluid. The only cure was to get him down fast. . . to more air pressure and more oxygen.

The trouble is, you can't get down *fast* from Base Camp on the north side of Everest.

Fortunately, the American team had a Gamov bag, a piece of equipment that could save Ric's life. A Gamov bag is eight feet long, and three-and-a-half feet high. We put Ric into it and zipped it up. Oxygen was fed in through the top. A foot pedal pumped air into the bag, like blowing up an air mattress. The goal was to increase the oxygen content and build up enough pressure in the bag to create an atmosphere equivalent to the environment our bodies normally operate in. Ric's body could then slowly recover.

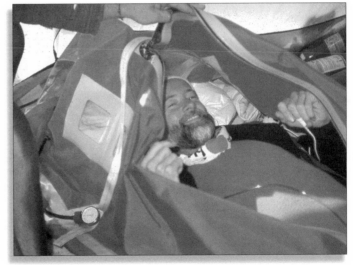

For eighteen hours, four of us took turns pumping the pedal and watching through a little window in the bag as Ric's life ebbed and flowed in front of us. His eyes would sink into his head, he would go grey, gurgle, and choke. Then the oxygen would hit and he'd come back.

After twelve hours, we decided he needed liquids. We reduced the pressure, took him out of the bag and gave him some liquid. Then he started to gurgle. He couldn't handle the loss in pressure and oxygen. We zipped him back up in the bag and frantically started pumping.

As I pumped and watched a friend and teammate who was probably going to die, I wondered what on earth I was doing on this mountain!

Yesterday, Ric was fine. Today, through no fault of his own, he was on the verge of death. As I pumped, questions whirled through my mind: What motivates me? At the very core of me, what is it that makes me do things? What do I value? What are my *values?*

What motivates me?

What do I value?

What are my values?

Watching him enabled me to see clearly that values were the essence of all motivation and all decisions. Great philosophers have, I'm sure, realized this before, but I had to figure it out for myself. And I had to be put in a black and white situation to realize the importance of understanding myself and my values.

So, as I pumped, I thought.

Competition and challenge. These words have always been at my core. Tell me I can't do it and I'll respond. My high school guidance counsellor said I wasn't smart enough to go to university. I went, and graduated with straight As, a Merit Award, and a Fellowship offer. After my first interview, the human resources manager at Procter & Gamble said they wouldn't hire me. I persisted. I got the job. I bought the family advertising agency from my father and brothers and a bunch of us took it from number twenty-two in the industry to one of the top three. The prevailing attitude in the industry was that only the big agencies in New York or London could build international groups and that Canadians couldn't. By the time we finished, we had options or agreements to buy businesses in twenty-eight countries.

I became Chairman of Outward Bound Canada. I created The Hayhurst Career Centre, which provides counselling on an experiential rather than psychological base, something that, to my knowledge, had never been done in this industry before. Hundreds of clients have told us we've helped to change their lives, and to build their confidence.

Challenge, I believed, was my first value. Challenge motivates me. But if that was so, why was I having second thoughts about *this* challenge, probably the greatest challenge I'd ever faced? Was there something more basic that drives me, a deeper core value?

I dug deeper. I tested my operating style and my decision-making methods. I looked for situations in which I felt most satisfied in a pure sense, not where someone else, a parent, a teacher, a boss, said I'd done well, but where I felt I'd done a great job.

I found another phrase. *Control of my own destiny* seemed more important than challenge. Perhaps it was my core value, deeper than challenge. To be in control of situations, not totally in a spiritual sense, but just of those things that I could make decisions about. When I was in control, when I got to make the final decision, I was really motivated . . . and did my best work.

Was there something

more basic that drives me,

a deeper core value?

When I was a travelling salesman for Procter & Gamble, one store owner refused to discuss our products with me despite the fact that I sold the number one brands in four categories. He hated Procter & Gamble. I knew my boss would tell me not to leave the store until he had bought from me, but I didn't think that was the right way to deal with him. I just dropped in every two weeks for three months, said "Hi" and tried to start a conversation about anything, just trying to build a rapport. Finally, the day before my boss was coming to show me how to handle the account, my patient style paid off and I made a huge sale. I did it my way. I maintained control of my destiny. I loved the feeling.

No wonder I was having second thoughts about this climb. Yesterday Ric was fine; today, through no fault of his own, his system has collapsed. He was no longer in control. So neither was I!

I dug further. Was challenge then my second value? No, I thought, it was probably my *family*. I tested this against this situation. Would my kids stop loving me if I quit, turned around, came back down? No.

My core values served as a template to test the climb against. I was able to decide, then and there, that at the slightest sign of any trouble, at the slightest change in control or risk to my family, I would quit. Leave the team. Give up. Chicken out.

Words I had never used before. But they were comfortable in my mind now as I stood pumping Ric's bag. I knew my *core values* and I would use them to make tough decisions. Without regret or second thoughts.

Core Values—Vital Signposts of Life

If you don't figure out what is at your core, what you stand for, and what ultimately motivates you, you'll always second-guess yourself. You'll always have regrets. Uncover your core values and use them as a template to test decisions in your life.

CHAPTER 29

A Second Death

Crystallizes the Message

After eighteen hours, one of the members of the American team brought us grim news: we had to get Ric out of the bag; an American needed it. We did the next best thing we could. We put Ric on straight oxygen and Carl and John started down the mountain with him. Back to Lhasa and to medical help. (Weeks later we learned that the altitude change and direct oxygen he got in Lhasa cleared the edema. Ric was fine.)

Again we were plagued by doubts. We stared at the mountain, searching for an answer. Were these omens? After two days, we decided to continue preparing to climb. We worked out on the mountain.

Then two days later, Benoît came to visit again. *Another climber had died.* There had been five of them within 600 vertical feet of the peak of Everest. They could see the top! But the climbing leader had decided they had to turn around and go back. The weather was closing in and he didn't think they could get to the top and safely back down again.

Michel, one of the climbers, said he wasn't going to leave. All his life he had dreamed of Everest. Now he could see the peak. He was going on, no matter what the rest did.

Now, you don't spend a lot of time arguing on a ridge that's over 28,000 feet. He said he was going on; they said they were going back. That was that. They gave him a walkie-talkie and some supplies, and they headed back down. Every now and then over the next 26 hours, he would report in. Then they lost touch. A day later an avalanche came down the couloir (a large funnel-shaped gully) he was climbing. No one knew if he had died in the avalanche or before it, but he was surely dead.

Again Benoît and I went for a walk. I asked him about Michel.

"He was my best friend. A superb climber. He would head off by himself and climb for hours in Europe, the toughest rock and ice faces. He believed in himself completely. He trusted his judgement more than anyone else's."

I suggested that, like Pierre, Michel was not on The Right Mountain.

"What do you mean this time?"

"He trusted his judgement more than anyone else's," I explained. His core value, I realized, was much like my own. "He wanted to be in control of his own destiny! But he couldn't be in complete control of himself on this mountain, and it is almost impossible to climb Everest alone. If he had compared this core value of trusting himself completely with the needs of the mountain, he would have realized there was no match. He would then have either modified his behaviour or stayed off the mountain. He didn't, and it cost him his life."

We had a moment of silence for Michel and each of us thought of the consequences of not knowing who you are—your *core values*—before making decisions.

Back here, in real life, you don't die if you don't know these core values, and use them as a template for decision making. Or do you? In a job, a relationship, or any situation, if you don't have a solid basis for making decisions, a template that is forged in experience, you'll make wrong decisions and you'll second-guess yourself. You'll be unsatisfied. And if you are *unsatisfied*, you won't be *motivated*. And if you are not *motivated*, you won't be *successful*. And if you are not successful, you'll get fired, or dumped and you'll wither and, metaphorically, die.

It is as important here, as it is on the mountain, to know your *core values*.

How do you uncover them, the real ones? Well, you could go to Everest. Or you could sit down and dig quietly into what motivates you. (That's what the exercises at the back of this book are for.) But somehow you have to find out who you really are.

It is as important here, as it is on the mountain, to know your core values.

The Right Mountain

You have to know your core values to choose the right mountain for you.

CHAPTER 30

Final Preparations
for the Climb to the Peak

This second death didn't

have the same impact. I

hated to think I was

valuing life less.

gain we stared at the mountain. Did we dare continue to climb? Once again we mused and then slowly started to talk. Yes, we would continue.

It was strange. This second death didn't have the same impact on me as the first one. The decision to continue on was easier. Was I getting jaded? Was it simply that it had occurred farther away, physically? Was I oxygen deprived? Was I becoming inured? Or maybe I had begun to feel that "these things happen." I hated to think that I was valuing life less. Perhaps, I decided, it was just that I understood the risks better. Maybe I knew myself better and knew where to draw the line for myself! I knew my *core values* and was confident in my decision-making ability.

We got ready to go on. At this stage, the roles were definite. Barry and Marc were going to attempt the summit; John, Hank, Dixon, and Carl had support roles above Base Camp; the rest of us were basically porters, carrying supplies up to the Advance Camp, if we could. We laid out all the equipment in order of priority. You see, you can't always take everything up the mountain, but you have to be sure to take the essentials. The good news was that Barry and Marc weren't taking ropes, ice screws, or oxygen, all heavy and bulky items.

Life off the mountain has priorities too, but often we don't take the time to establish them. We worry about everything: the economy, the safety of our cities, the weather. They aren't essential to our day-to-day lives, so they shouldn't take up a lot of our thinking time. We should focus on the relevant stuff. The black-and-white, life-and-death situation of the mountain makes the assignment of priorities easier. It is tougher back home where so many issues face us, but still it must be done.

We started filling our packs and testing our loads. The next question was, "How much can we carry?" If we took too much, the extra weight could keep us from reaching the top. If, on the other hand, we lightened our load, we might be missing vital life-saving supplies. Finally, we all found loads we were comfortable with and we started out. Jimmy had about eighty pounds on his back. Jim Law about seventy pounds.

Establishing Priorities

How much can you carry in your life, in a job, as a volunteer? You have to prioritize. There is no shame in carrying a lighter pack. The only shame is in saying you'll do it, and not doing it.

CHAPTER 31

I Have to Turn Back

*M*other Nature struck again. We had been climbing for four hours when suddenly Dixon began to hemorrhage. Blood poured out of his nose. We rushed to him. The altitude had caused epistaxis (a nosebleed). The only cure was to get him back to a lower altitude.

Initially, all we could do was stuff toilet paper to stop the flow of blood. Then two of the strongest climbers, John and Hank, took him back to Base Camp. There, the flow slowed down and stopped, but he knew he was through climbing. He agreed to stay at Base Camp to co-ordinate efforts from there.

The rest of the team went on.

Just below the area called the Ice Pinnacles, we stopped for a rest and some food and liquid. I sat down. My head ached. I asked Carl to come over. He examined me.

"I'm afraid it's cerebral edema," he said. "You have to go down."

I agreed immediately.

Two guys volunteered to start back down with me. After a couple of hours into our descent I told them I felt better.

"You two should go back," I said.

"No, we're staying with you," Hank said.

Two hours later, when I made the same suggestion, they agreed to go back up to the team. They took the "priority" stuff—oxygen and fuel—out of my pack and they left me with the lesser priority items from their packs. I went on alone. It took me six hours to get back to Base Camp.

Physically it was hell. I had lost the adrenalin that comes with the climb, the goal, and I became aware of all my aches and pains. By that time, I had worn the toe nails off five of my toes. Every step, every footfall rubbed the raw, bleeding flesh against the end of my boot.

Mentally it was easy. From that moment to this day, I have not had a second thought. No "if only;" no "Maybe I should have. . . ." I know I made the right decision. I know because I laid my *core values* down on top of the decision and there was a perfect match. The decision to go on would have been in direct conflict with *control of my own destiny.* The cerebral edema was not something I had any control over. The cost of going on could have been my life.

From that moment on I have had no trouble telling people that I quit, I gave up, I chickened out. I have told my family and my friends; I have said it in the over 250 public speeches I have given throughout North America, Mexico, and Europe. Never once have I had a second thought, because I knew and believed totally in my *core values* and their priority ranking.

And from that moment on these *core values* have been

. . . core values have been my

yardstick, my template

as I make decisions

in my life.

my yardstick, my template, as I make decisions in my personal, business, and volunteer life. I no longer feel badly when I say no to going on the United Way board, because large volunteer boards don't match my *core values* of control of my destiny. But give me a United Way project, an assignment, and I'll gladly undertake it and give it my all.

I now know why I've been my own boss in business for so long: I work better that way. I would not be a great employee unless I had control of my destiny.

I know my family relationship works because both my wife and I are independent. We both let the other have control of our own destinies. We would not have as strong a marriage if I had to be home at 6:30 every night and she was dependent on me or needed control over me. She has her own life, and we have a life together and with our children.

Knowing who you are means you have a template for life's decisions. This template increases confidence and minimizes the "maybe I should have" and the "if only."

Decision Making

Understanding your core values makes

decisions easy. When you know who you are,

you can make confident decisions and never

second-guess yourself.

CHAPTER 32

Jimmy Hits the Wall

ut the team went on, carrying vital supplies up to the 21,000-foot level for Barry and Marc to use as a base for their final push.

They were just over 20,000 feet when Jimmy fell to his knees and screamed. As he looked up, he could see an area only six inches wide. He had tunnel vision. Then when he put his arm up to get out of his pack, he found he had no control over it. He was totally disoriented.

He had vicious cerebral edema.

Barry and Marc heard his scream and scurried back to him. They recognized the problem right away and started him back down the mountain. I had been back at Base Camp for two nights and the better part of three days when I saw Jimmy being helped back down. I knew he had a serious problem, but at least he seemed mobile.

I grabbed him and held him. I looked into his eyes; they were glazed. He smiled wanly.

He sat down. He lay down. He went to sleep. I watched his chest rise and fall. I prayed. I'm probably an agnostic, but I still prayed. I don't remember what I said.

My mind raced through all the possibilities: Cerebral edema had killed Pierre; the bag had at least temporarily worked for Ric. Could we get down fast enough? What if he died? Would we have to cremate him? I couldn't go home without him, on and on and on. I had started this, I caused his death, we had promised his mother we wouldn't separate . . . on and on. He was just a kid; I knew we shouldn't have done this, I shouldn't have let him go on; I should have set some guidelines, he should have set some guidelines. Didn't he feel it coming? What were his core values? On and on.

Within hours, which seemed like days, he was feeling a little better. Carl, who had stayed with Dixon at Base Camp, said Jimmy was going to be okay. I slept, exhausted.

The next day he was feeling much better, the headaches had subsided, his vision was back and he had control of his limbs. I saw him staring up at the mountain. His face reflected a gamut of emotions: awe, fear, anger, respect. He had been through a life-changing experience.

Years later, someone asked Jimmy what his experience had meant, how it had changed him. He replied that something had happened on Everest. He had grown up in a fairly well-to-do family, and he had expected to go into business and live the same way his parents did. In fact, most of his friends were materially oriented and building a corporate lifestyle.

By facing death, he found his *core values*. He came to understand life and what was important to him. He made some life-changing decisions. He now runs a charity, Trails Youth Initiatives in Toronto, working with vulnerable kids from the inner city, helping to give them a chance at life. He knows he'll never make big bucks doing this, but it is more important to him to help these kids than to buy a Porsche. Interestingly, a bunch of his peers have put together a fundraising group for Trails; they think he's doing a neat thing, too. They are touching one of their values by helping others.

When Jimmy was asked how he thought the climb had changed his dad, his reply was superb, better than anything I had thought of: "Dad used to challenge death. Now I think he respects life."

Using Core Values

When you know who you are, you can make

confident decisions for yourself, and you can

define success in your own terms, rather

than letting your parents, your peers, or

society define it.

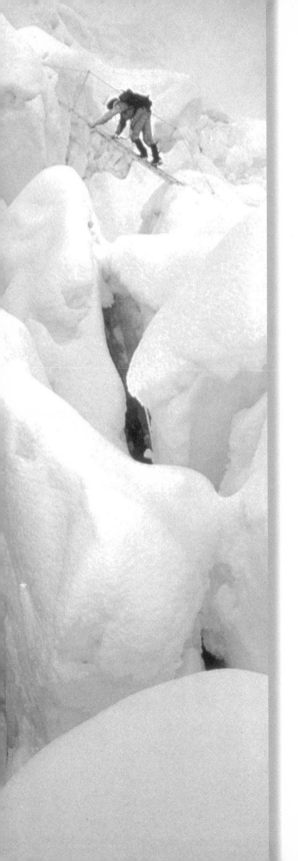

CHAPTER 33

The Team Goes On

The team went on without Jimmy and me. I wondered what lay ahead. I remembered some of the obstacles that the 1986 expedition had faced. Among the worst were the ice crevasses, some fifteen feet deep, others 200 feet deep. You cross them by placing an aluminum extension ladder (you have to carry it up there!) across the crevasse, digging it into the ice, tying a rope around your waist, and crawling across. The rope is there to bring back the body if the ladder slips and you fall; so you spend a lot of time digging the base of the ladder into the ice before you start across!

And there is an ice ridge over a mile in width. To cross it in Everest's gusty winds, they used ropes and ice screws. Ice screws are like those things we use in the backyard to tie the dog up. You know, you screw it into the ground, tie the rope to it, tie the other end to the dog. Same thing on the mountain. You screw it into the ice, tie a rope to it, tie the rope to yourself, and walk slowly across.

The question is: How far apart do you put the ice screws? If you go forty or fifty yards and a 150 mile-per-hour wind comes up, you could be blown off the side and killed. If, on the other hand, as is my inclination, you put an ice screw in every six inches, you can't carry enough ice screws to cross the ridge.

Security and Support Systems

How solid is the base of your ladder? How secure are you, in your knowledge base, your technical skills, your people support systems? If you are not secure, you can fall down or get blown away. In school, if you get promoted without basic language skills, it always catches up to you. If you job-hop to get ahead, but don't know the fundamentals, you can trip and fall.

How far is it between the ice screws — the security points — in your life? In your relationships, your job, your family?

CHAPTER 34

The Final Assault

inally the team, now reduced to two climbers and two support team members, reached the Advance Camp. It was just a couple of tents on a flat ledge, with fuel, stoves, food, and a walkie-talkie. From here on, Barry and Marc would go alone, each carrying thirty pounds. They were going to climb for forty hours (forty!). They would be going up a steep couloir that had never been successfully climbed before. They would use their ice axes and crampons to climb slowly, a foot at a time.

At the top of the couloir was a ridge that had to be crossed to get to the vertical face that was the last 1,800 feet to the peak of Everest. They would stop here for six hours to rest and drink, then go on for another six hours.

If they weren't at the summit by then, they'd have to turn back. Their bodies wouldn't be able take any more. From 25,000 feet on, your body deteriorates, it eats its own muscle and cartilage to stay alive. Your brain cells deteriorate. Your thinking skills falter. There is nothing you can do about it.

Four times, Barry and Marc tried to summit. Once, Barry got cerebral edema. Once he got pulmonary edema. And on one attempt, Marc's feet got too cold to continue. Each time, they returned to Base Camp for about a week, re-acclimatized, then tried again.

On the fourth attempt, they were again forced back. They realized that, even if they made it to the top, they wouldn't make it back down again.

It wasn't worth it. They didn't try again.

Everest Express did not make it to the top of Everest.

But did we succeed? I guess you get to decide.

I believe success is personal, it is individual, it should not be a societal evaluation. If you try to live by others' rules, you'll never be satisfied or feel successful, because there will always be someone richer, more beautiful, more talented, stronger, more successful than you.

Personally, and as a team, we felt successful. We all had personal bests. We climbed a couloir that had never been climbed before. We all lived. And we learned, individually and collectively.

I learned about *core values.*

I learned about choosing The Right Mountain.

Dr. Viktor E. Frankl says, "Success, like happiness, cannot be pursued, it must ensue, and it only does so as the unintended side effect of one's personal dedication to a cause greater than oneself or as the by-product of one's surrender to a person other than oneself."

I also learned about the Right Vista.

I got to 17,800 feet, Jimmy got just over 20,000 feet, Hank got to over 22,000 feet, Barry and Marc to 28,000 feet. If I had gone any farther, I might have died. If Jimmy had gone any farther, he could have died.

To know

The Right Mountain

and to recognize The

Right Vista, you have to

know yourself,

your core values.

Two French climbers, Pierre and Michel, had died.

Our society says you have to keep climbing up, up the hierarchical ladder to the top, to be successful. Start as a teacher, become a department head, a vice-principal, then a principal. Start as a salesperson, become a district manager, then vice-president of sales. Climb the ladder, make more money. Get to the top!

That's a crock. You don't have to keep climbing up the hierarchical or financial ladder, or any other one. For each of us there is a level, a limit. If you go beyond it, well, you won't die, but you'll fail, and wither and die, metaphorically. We should figure out who we are, what we are good at, and do that. We shouldn't let bosses or society or peers push us into something that isn't a good match, a good fit, for our skills, our interests, and our values.

To know The Right Mountain and to recognize The Right Vista, you have to know yourself, your *core values*. *Core values* are the key to personal success, to feeling good, having fun, and looking back on the decisions in your life without regrets.

That's what I learned, or perhaps saw more clearly, on The Right Mountain.

What Is the Definition of Success?

TRUE SUCCESS

is the attainment of purpose

without compromising

CORE VALUES

I hope you enjoyed the trip.

Jim Haghurt Sr

SUCCESS

My definition of success is:

_____

_____

_____

_____

_____

_____

_____

_____

_____

NEXT STEPS

Now that you've finished this book, you can sit back, relax, and just remember the story. Or you can treat it as a learning experience, and do some exercises.

Your choice.

If you want to go on, turn to the next page. And if you want to climb higher, learn more, continue the exercises.

Whatever your decision, I hope you enjoyed *The Right Mountain.*

E X E R C I S E I

What metaphors do I remember from *The Right Mountain?*

1._____

_____

_____

2._____

_____

_____

3._____

_____

_____

4._____

_____

_____

5._____

_____

_____

6._____

_____

_____

Any others?

_____

_____

_____

_____

_____

_____

_____

If this exercise has whetted your appetite and you want to learn more about yourself, how to make better decisions, have fewer regrets, and generally get more out of life, move on to the next exercises. They're fun. They take some introspection, but they are very rewarding.

If you want to dig further, if you want to dig out your core values, if you want to develop a *template* for your life, for your definition of *success,* start Exercise II.

EXERCISE II

After re-reading or skimming through the book again, what other metaphors, messages do I remember?

1._____

_____

_____

2._____

_____

_____

3._____

_____

_____

What anecdotes or incidents in my life do these metaphors and the ones in Exercise I trigger in my life?

Example: Leeches. Those little things that irritate you, that aren't important, but that you have to control or they will control you.

• I remember how upset I used to get because nobody in our house put the dirty dishes in the dishwasher. When I look back, it wasn't really important. I wasted a lot of energy on that.

- The paperwork I have to go through regularly to get approvals to minor expenses drives me crazy and I fuss and complain about it every month. I can't change it, so why don't I just stop worrying about it. It is not going to change the world!

List Anecdotes:

- _____

  _____

- _____

  _____

- _____

  _____

- _____

  _____

Now that I have identified them, can I put them aside and not let them bug me? Can I at least try to?

Every time I'm irritated, I'll ask myself: *Is this going to change the world or is this just a leech?*

EXERCISE III

*Value. Values. What are your values and how do you prioritize them? Discovering them, analyzing them, and priorizing them will help define **success** for you.*

The following exercises are a catalyst. They help discipline you through the process of discovering, articulating, and priorizing your *values*.

Typically, the questions take a while to answer. The first attempts are often just that . . . first attempts. Usually some "steeping" time and "digging" are required to find real truths. Focus, a clear mind, no time limits, and no interruptions, usually uncover the essences we're looking for in our search.

CORE VALUES

We are looking for experiences in our lives when we really felt *complete*, when we cared about what we had done, when we did it for its *own sake*, not for any predetermined, ulterior motive. The experience usually will be described with a *problem*, an *action*, and a *result*, that gave the satisfaction. It will be a personally rewarding experience.

In order to get breadth and thus a total *life* definition, rather than just a *career* definition, we are looking for a meaningful experience in each of five areas of our lives.

Listed below are the areas, arbitrarily designated, and examples of experiences to get you thinking.

1. Career/Job/Home

Example: Bobby was afraid of the water because his brother had drowned the previous summer, and told me, his counsellor, that he was not going to swim. During the two months at summer camp, I worked with Bobby, getting him to play in the water, splash, dive, and finally he was playing waterpolo. He left camp smiling, forgetting that he had said he'd never swim. I felt I'd made a real difference.

Bill was going to quit our company and start his own research firm. Rather than try to talk him out of it, I discussed the joys and frustrations of entrepreneurship. Eventually he felt he'd be better off with a non-active partner, or mentor. We set up the company as a joint venture and it prospered for both of us.

2. Volunteer Activities

Example: Peter wanted me to join his charity's board. I knew I wasn't great on boards, so I tried to talk him into finding a project I could work on rather than a board role. We soon realized that the organization needed a Strategic Review. I led several board members through the review which resulted in both a repositioning and a real board commitment to the new strategy.

3. EDUCATION

Example: In university, I had to take a statistics course. After four weeks, I was lost. I went to the professor and he agreed I was out of my depth. He was astounded when I said I hadn't taken any math for three years and said I wouldn't be able to pass the course without that background. But I had to! On my own, I analyzed the course, set up a study program, got tutoring, and aced the exam. I loved the feeling!

4. EXTRA-CURRICULAR

Example: My high school and university gang rented a hockey rink for an hour twice a week the year we all started working. It kept the gang together, we relived our memories and it was exercise. But I found it cut into both my family and my work time. Unlike some of the others, I couldn't do all three. I had to decide how to manage my time. I fretted long and hard, but finally gave up hockey. I missed the camaraderie. They're still playing 30 years later, but I made the right decision for me.

5. PERSONAL

Example: While Chairman of an organization including 8 companies and over 400 employees, I found it difficult to keep in touch with my kids. Because their boarding schools were close to my office, I put a note on my desk that urged me, if I had a free hour, to drive to one of their schools, even if just to say hi. One day I arrived just as my son was elected Captain of the First Soccer team. I was standing off to the side and he was unaware of my presence when the vote was announced. I cherish that moment.

Now it's your turn. Take the time to review experiences in your life that have really struck a chord with you. In each of the categories, detail one of the most meaningful times you have had. It may be wise to get an exercise book to write your musings in because the experiences will be revised, reviewed, and sometimes thrown out over the course of time.

EXPERIENCES

1. CAREER/JOB/HOME

_____

_____

_____

_____

_____

_____

2. VOLUNTEER ACTIVITIES

_____

_____

_____

_____

_____

_____

3. EDUCATION

_____

_____

_____

_____

_____

_____

4. EXTRA-CURRICULAR

_____

_____

_____

_____

_____

_____

5. PERSONAL

_____

_____

_____

_____

_____

_____

Review, modify, rewrite these events until you have them in a written form that truly captures the essence of your experience.

Then go on to Exercise IV.

E X E R C I S E   I V

Now we will look for the *values* that these experiences both denote and connote. Each of these experiences is important to you and the *value* words will help clarify why.

Listed below are some *value* words. To list is to omit, so look for any words that might be missed on this basic list.

Advancement	Income	Satisfaction
Authority	Independence	Security
Autonomy	Integrity	Spirituality
Camaraderie	Leadership	Stability
Challenge	Leisure Activities	Status
Contribution to	Merit	Variety
Society	Personal Growth	Wealth
Control	Power	
Family	Prestige	
Freedom	Relationships	
Fun	Respect	
Health	Responsibility	
Helping Others	Risk	

Example: Teaching Bobby how to swim.

> Values: Autonomy, Challenge, Control, Freedom, Helping Others, Independence, Integrity, Leadership, Personal Relationships, Responsibility, Risk, Sales Factor.

Example: Peter's Board

> Values: Autonomy, Challenge, Control, Freedom, Helping Others, Independence, Risk.

Now, fill in the *value* words that occur in each of your designated Experiences.

1. Career/Job/Home

_____

_____

_____

_____

_____

2. Volunteer Activities

_____

_____

_____

_____

_____

3. EDUCATION

_____

_____

_____

_____

_____

_____

4. EXTRA-CURRICULAR

_____

_____

_____

_____

_____

_____

5. PERSONAL

_____

_____

_____

_____

_____

_____

Review each list at least once to see if any *values* have been missed. Add words to the list where appropriate. Let them *steep.*

E X E R C I S E   V

Now, review each list, looking for words, *values*, that have appeared twice or more.

1._____ 5._____

2._____ 6._____

3._____ 7._____

4._____ 8._____

These are *core values*, values that occur again and again in experiences that are truly meaningful to you.

Now, priorize them. List them in order.

1._____

2._____

3._____

4._____

Now test the priority. Test against day-to-day experiences. For example, if *family* occurs on that list, what does that mean? Regular dinners, good-night kisses, being at your child's play? It is *your* definition, but you have to *define* it, to *live* it. If *wealth* is on the list, what does it mean, specifically? If *freedom* is there, what does it mean?

- How often do you achieve the *priority* you, yourself put on this *value?*

- Is it a wish or a real priority in your life?

- Does the list need re-priorizing because it was a *"wish list"* of priorities not a *"real life"* list of priorities?

Make a list, locking in and absolutely confirming the top three or four—usually we can't handle more than three or four as a basis for decision making. When you feel you have truly articulated your *core values*, write them on a card and put it in your wallet. Write them on the note board in the kitchen. Write them on your daily organizer.

Now *live* the *list*, live the priorities. If you make decisions based on them, you won't be second-guessing yourself. You will live your life by your *core values*. See if you don't have *fewer regrets;* if the phrases *if only, maybe I should have,* if the second-guessing doesn't start to disappear from your life.

TRUE SUCCESS

is the attainment of purpose

without compromising

CORE VALUES

I hope this book and these exercises will help you squeeze more out of life. The true impact will be its lasting effects, rather than an immediate, yet temporary, change of behaviour. The inward achievement of self-control, rather than letting others implicitly or explicitly define your life, will give you the greatest freedom and most satisfying accomplishment of your life, because you'll know who you are and what you can and want to do.

T H A N K S

To The Everest Express Team:

Barry Blanchard, Chris Considine, Tom Christie, Gary Gault, Jeff Goguen, Dr. Carl Hannigan, Jim Hayhurst, Jr., Jim Law, Archie Louis, John Morel, Ric Singleton, Dixon Thompson, Marc Twight, Hank Van Weelden.

To Al, who started our Hayhurst business in Calgary, and got me involved with Everest.

To Ian, who invited me on my first Outward Bound expedition.

To John and The Fitness Institute staff, who trained my body and mind.

To those who went to Everest before and left a library of insights in books, tapes, and movies.

To Irene, who gave me insight and encouragement after my first feeble attempts at writing.

To Kurt Hahn, the creator of Outward Bound, whose axiom of "I don't have the energy to overcome the inertia of tradition" gave me the confidence to not "go where the path may lead, but to make my own trail in case others may wish to follow."

To *The Right Mountain* audiences, for the ideas they have given me as they heard the presentation, and for the personal growth that has resulted.

To all the suppliers and donors who helped make Everest Express possible.

To friends, for their patience as they heard the story over and over again.

To John, whose financial and people skills helped Hayhurst Advertising become a valuable asset which, when we sold it, enabled me to follow other dreams with a degree of financial security.

To Chris, who showed me my spiritual side, and is a patient and positive business partner and friend.

To Peter, who co-founded Trails Youth Initiatives with me, and opened up my eyes to the opportunities to give of yourself to help others.

To Paddy, whose research helped me find direction for the book.

To Frank, whose patient mentoring enabled me to recognize many of the metaphors in this book.

To "Wylie," who has always helped me keep perspective.

To Bill, who took some rambling thoughts and helped me organize them.

To Wendy, an Outward Bounder and true friend who has helped me see, understand, and believe in myself. She also helped Jimmy and me articulate our common values as we started Trails.

Especially to Gay, for her patience, encouragement, insights, questions, and belief in what I do—in my speeches, in my counselling, and in my book. And for the finger-breaking typing and re-typing.

To Caroline, who believed in the concept and pursued it.

To Jennifer, who was right when she made me rewrite.

To Karen, who got others at Wiley to believe in the project, kept me believing in it, and accommodated my idiosyncrasies.

To Cid, who said I could write, and does so herself, in a more disciplined and creative form.

To Boo, who said I may be a big shot when I stand on the stage, but when I'm in the big brown truck with our three dogs, I'm just her Dad.

To Jim Jr., who watched me fall down and helped me get up and grow as a man.

To Mum, whose adventurous genes I obviously inherited. In her seventies, she went heli-hiking and did a driver's skid-school course!

To Swebbs, who has always supported me, my ventures, and adventures, while keeping our house as a safe and warm haven for all of us.

AUTHOR'S NOTE

The Everest Express Team had a reunion in Calgary several months after our return to Canada. It was a black-tie dinner and we all brought our slides. You would think we had all been on different climbs! Each mini slide show was from a different perspective: Jimmy's focused entirely on people; Barry's on the climbing; John's on the physical beauty. Everyone had his individual view of the trip. That was when I truly realized that all of us see things, even the same things, through our own eyes, through our own experiences and predilections. My trip up Everest was different than each of the other team member's.

As a result, my interpretation of this particular trip—embodied in my speech and in this book—has to be different than that of each member of the Team. Not only do we remember the same incident differently, but we even focus on different incidents. Combine that with the lack of oxygen, the exhaustion, and the fact that "time heals all wounds," and you soon realize that recall of particular incidents cannot be perfectly clear; thus, logic and guess-work have to fill some of the gaps. If there are mistakes in fact, they are mine and mine alone, and I apologize. Several team members, and others who have been on Everest climbs, have heard my presentation and confirm the essences. But I know the past is almost as much a wink of the imagination as the future!

Most professional mountain climbers, particularly those who go to Everest, return to give motivational speeches; many have made successful full-time careers out of their experience. Others use the speeches to support their climbing lifestyle. As Barry says, mountain climbing is a "calling" that a lot of people dedicate themselves to with the same devotion that I do to my family. I am obviously not a professional mountain climber, but I have tremendous respect for those who are, and for the lessons that can be learned from physical challenges attempted, and understood.

The photographs, which are much of the live presentation and, I hope, an added benefit to this book, are either Jimmy's or mine for the most part. And we don't know which are which, except that he carried a big camera with several lenses and I carried a little two-stage pocket camera—it was lighter! The other photos were given to me by other team members or by Jim Elzinga, leader of the 1986 Expedition. I trust I haven't offended anyone by using their shots to crystallize the point I am trying to make.

Obviously, this climb had a huge impact on me, and on Jimmy. I have, I believe, unique friendships with our daughters Cid and Boo, as well as with Jimmy. I feel proud and blessed by these relationships. Everest changed Jimmy's and my relationship, as he saw his father fall down and, usually, get up. And I saw him grow and gain the wisdom that can only come with experience. I am Chairman of his charity, Trails Youth Initiatives, and we have a special relationship that works for both of us and for the kids we serve. This could not have happened without Everest.

We don't know whether this book will sell ten copies or ten thousand or perhaps more. But it would not have happened, and could not have happened, without each member of my family.

Thank you, the reader, for your support by buying this book. My mission, my goal in life, the focus of all I do, is to try to *make a difference* in someone else's life. Perhaps this book will make a difference in yours.

Thousands have heard the story of *The Right Mountain* through the live presentation. Many have said it has changed their lives.

I wrote this book for those who want to review the lessons from *The Right Mountain* in greater detail, at their own pace. I also wrote it so that many others can share the messages from *The Right Mountain* without seeing the presentation. I hope it is a catalyst that causes you to think and to grow.

Many have told us their stories of how *The Right Mountain* has affected them, in both their personal and professional lives. We would love to hear from you with your story. Just phone, write, fax or e-mail us at the address below.

If you would like to order more books, an audio or video tape of the live presentation, or an Everest poster; or if you would like information on the live presentation of *The Right Mountain*, simply call, write, or fax us at:

The Right Mountain
378 Fairlawn Avenue, Toronto, Ontario • M5M 1T8
Tel: 416-785-7700 • Fax: 416-785-3854
E-Mail: jim@therightmountain.com
Home Page: www.therightmountain.com

About The Author

Jim Hayhurst is a father of three, and a successful business executive. Under his leadership, the Hayhurst Group of Companies grew to become one of the top three advertising agencies in Canada. He was also Chairman of Outward Bound Canada. In 1987, he founded The Hayhurst Career Centre, an organization that helps people squeeze more satisfaction out of life.

In 1988, he participated in the Everest expedition that would change his life. He put together a slide show of his journey, and soon came to realize that this was much more than a travel story. He began to compare his experiences on the mountain with the challenges we all face in daily life, and found that his Everest climb was a powerful metaphor for defining success. Gradually, a valuable message took shape. He called that message *The Right Mountain*. Today, Jim Hayhurst presents *The Right Mountain* speech and slide show to businesses and organizations around the world, helping to change the lives of others.